Courageous
influence

More books by (in)courage

Take Heart: 100 Devotions to Seeing God When Life's Not Okay

LOOK FOR OTHER TITLES IN THIS SERIES:

Courageous Simplicity:
Abide in the Simple Abundance of Jesus

Courageous Joy:
Delight in God through Every Season

Courageous Influence:
Embrace the Way God Made You for Impact

Courageous Kindness:
Live the Simple Difference Right Where You Are
(October 2021)

For more resources, visit incourage.me.

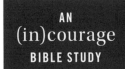
AN
(in)courage
BIBLE STUDY

courageous influence

EMBRACE THE WAY GOD MADE YOU FOR IMPACT

Written by Grace P. Cho
and the (in)courage Community

Revell
a division of Baker Publishing Group
Grand Rapids, Michigan

Published by Revell
a division of Baker Publishing Group
PO Box 6287, Grand Rapids, MI 49516-6287
www.revellbooks.com

Printed in the United States of America

Library of Congress Cataloging-in-Publication Data
Names: Cho, Grace P., editor.
Title: Courageous influence : embrace the way God made you for impact : (in) courage / edited by Grace P. Cho.
Description: Grand Rapids, Michigan : Revell, a division of Baker Publishing Group, [2021]
Identifiers: LCCN 2020049232 (print) | LCCN 2020049233 (ebook) | ISBN 9780800738105 (paperback) | ISBN 9780800740726 (casebound) | ISBN 9781493430512 (ebook)
Subjects: LCSH: Christian women—Religious life—Textbooks. | Influence (Psychology)—Religious aspects—Christianity—Textbooks.
Classification: LCC BV4527 .C6865 2021 (print) | LCC BV4527 (ebook) | DDC 248.8/43—dc23
LC record available at https://lccn.loc.gov/2020049232
LC ebook record available at https://lccn.loc.gov/2020049233

21 22 23 24 25 26 27   7 6 5 4 3 2 1

contents

introduction

In today's social media–saturated world, the word *influence* conjures up images of beautifully curated Instagram feeds or women who lead from the stage and have thousands of followers. It's measured by the number of likes and shares and how well we can get people to imitate us. Influence has almost become synonymous with fame and power, and if we're being honest, many of us long to have it.

But in its purest form, influence is simply the capacity to effect change in someone. It doesn't have the implications of celebrity culture or amassing power for self-promotion. It is the ability to impact others for a certain purpose. And from a biblical perspective, influence is the right and responsibility of everyone who follows Christ.

Like a stone thrown into the middle of a lake, our life in Christ should have ripple effects that reverberate from us to all those in our circles. Our faith is in a living God, and thus His movements should be evident in every part of our lives, throughout every season, and to everyone around us. It is a natural result of life in Him that people see how we've been impacted by Jesus, and it's our privilege to influence others to know Him too.

Influence isn't only for pastors and leaders in the church. It's not about having a position of power or years of experience. It has nothing to do with age or gender or how much clout we already have. All of us have been given influence in Christ, and we are to use it to encourage and lead others toward Him.

Influence will take on different forms for every person. It can look like using our gifts, skills, time, and effort. It can be about where God has placed us—our location or our proximity to someone else or the role we play in our families, jobs, and communities. We can influence others in ordinary ways, like having someone over for dinner or walking with them through grief, or in particular ways, like writing a book or leading a ministry.

Wherever we are, however God has made us, in Christ we are women of influence.

As we push against our culture's definition of influence, we will need courage. We will run into doubt and insecurity. Some people may discount our capacity and abilities. The call to impact others for God's kingdom might feel overwhelming. But that's why we're going to do this together.

Over the next six weeks, we will study God's Word and answer reflection questions that will help us put into practice what we're learning. Our faith should always have both a solid orthodoxy (what we believe) and a solid orthopraxy (how we live it out), and this Bible study aims to achieve both. *Courageous Influence* will guide you in the journey of living the impact you were made to have.

Let's turn the world's idea of influence on its head and become the courageous women of influence God calls us to be.

How to Use This Study

Courageous Influence is a great study for personal or small group use. If you're doing it with a group, we recommend allowing at least forty-five minutes for discussion, or more for larger groups. (We think groups of four to ten people work great!) Enhance your community study experience with our *Courageous Influence* leader guide and videos. Go to www.incourage.me/leaderguides to download your small group resources.

As you begin each day of this study, take a moment to be still and pray. Ask God to meet you, teach you, and convict you. Since there will be a lot of material to digest, take your time and feel free to go at your own pace.

Some days you will be asked to look up Scripture passages in different translations. Use www.biblegateway.com or a Bible app to reference those.

When you read through Bible passages, pay attention to word choice and repetition. If it's a narrative, try to imagine yourself in that story and ask, *What do I notice (setting, character, tone of voice, sequence of events, historical context)? What is God showing me about Himself? What is God showing me about myself?*

Use every inch of white space in this study to process your thoughts and to write out prayers, questions, and reflections.

Each week focuses on a different aspect of influence:

- **Week 1** begins with a foundational statement: You are a woman of influence.
- **Week 2** reveals that influence is about where God has placed you and your willingness to say yes to Him.
- **Week 3** explores what it means to be a person of integrity in using our influence.
- **Week 4** teaches us to be generous with our influence.
- **Week 5** shows us how to be intentional with our influence.
- **Week 6** explores how storytelling can be a powerful way of influencing others.

Each week has a cadence that will help you get the most out of this study:

- **Day 1** looks at our call to courageously explore that week's topic.
- **Day 2** tackles what the world says about that week's topic.
- **Day 3** spotlights how Jesus or another key biblical figure lived it out and what we can learn from that person.

- **Day 4** shows God's heart for you in that topic.
- **Day 5** closes the week with motivation for becoming a coura-geous woman of influence.

We at (in)courage are excited to begin this *Courageous Influence* journey with you. You'll see that each day opens with a story from one of our writers sharing her experience of living out her influence. We hope these stories will help you feel less alone and more inspired as you look for God in your own story.

Are you ready? Join us as we redefine what influence means and learn to impact others the way God made us to!

me? a woman of influence?

You are the salt of the earth. But if the salt should lose its taste, how can it be made salty? It's no longer good for anything but to be thrown out and trampled under people's feet.

You are the light of the world. A city situated on a hill cannot be hidden. No one lights a lamp and puts it under a basket, but rather on a lampstand, and it gives light for all who are in the house. In the same way, let your light shine before others, so that they may see your good works and give glory to your Father in heaven.

Matthew 5:13–16

My cheeks held on to the heat as it spread across my face. I fanned myself with my fingers to no avail. I'd just run up two flights of stairs to make it on time for a meeting with my creative writing professor. I took a deep breath before stepping into his office for the first time.

He sat at a large desk with a recent draft of my short story set before him. The scents and songs of my childhood, which I often found impossible to share in other places, felt at home typed into paragraphs. I sat down and put my backpack on my lap, then moved it down to the floor beneath my feet, then back up again.

Pointing to a shelf behind me, he asked if I'd read two particular books there. He listed the titles. I read the Asian words on the spine of one book and silently corrected his mispronunciation.

Thoughts so loud I was sure he could hear them immediately came to mind: *Don't correct him. You probably have the word wrong, even though you've lived in the Asian country it comes from. You aren't smart enough to be a writer.*

I hunched over my backpack, telling myself that my voice was best kept quiet, my stories were safer untold, and I was better off keeping to the shadows and margins.

As we continued to talk, the title he'd mispronounced accidentally slipped out of my mouth. He paused, hearing my correct pronunciation. He held up my story in his hands and said, "You are doing something in all of your writing that I cannot teach. Your writing is powerful." Then he said, "And why in the world didn't you correct me on the pronunciation of that title earlier?" I shrugged, feeling the heat rush back to my cheeks.

That meeting took place over twenty years ago. It was the birth of a belief that perhaps my voice, stories, womanhood, experiences, and ethnicity matter, not just in silent spaces of prayer or as tiny afterthoughts of my identity but as main characters that were intentionally given to help tell the story of God's image and glory.

That day God spoke through my professor, saying, *Stop hiding the stories I have given you. Let Me use your voice to reveal My heart and light.*

—TASHA JUN

Can you remember a time when you tried to make yourself smaller in an effort to hide? What prompted you to do so?

I was in a bible study in B'ham and I felt everyone in the room was so deep (mature) in their faith. I felt like a baby in my faith. I was scared to open my mouth.

Throughout life, our interactions with others shape the way we think about ourselves. Messages we hear from our culture, our parents, and our peers set the standard for what is considered worthy and beautiful. On the flip side, we also begin to understand what is considered shameful and ugly by the negative looks and words we receive.

Those categories create labels that we attach to certain areas of our lives. We dissect our bodies, thoughts, and desires, and we label them as good or bad, valuable or useless. In doing so, we learn to have an incongruent and unbalanced view of who we are. On the one hand, we strive to puff up the parts of ourselves that seem approved by others, but on the other hand, we try to cover up or silence the parts that seem unacceptable or uncool.

Instead of being whole, we become fractured.

Instead of being the light of the world, we become dim and unseen.

Instead of being the salt of the earth, we become bland and our voices go unheard.

Fractured. Unseen. Unheard. This is not who we were made to be.

We were made to shine, to have our good works bring glory to God. We were made to have influence, to have an effect on those around us and on this world *because* we have been made new in Christ.

> **We were made to have influence, to have an effect on those around us and on this world because we have been made new in Christ.**

As women who have been changed by Jesus's life, death, and resurrection, we aren't meant to hide any part of who we are. As Matthew 5:15 says, "No one lights a lamp and puts it under a basket, but rather on a lampstand, and it gives light for all who are in the house." We are meant to be seen, to be fully who we were made to be, because God desires to show Himself to the world through our whole selves.

What are the labels you've put on yourself—your body, your mind, and even your spiritual life? What parts of your life have you deemed good

or bad, valuable or useless? Write down every word you can think of that
has had a positive or negative impact on your identity.

— low reader group = not very smart
My mother's confidence
+ On the Good Ship Lollypop = before others.
+time
+ Hospitality · Useful - creative, learner, cook

Read Philippians 2:1–18. As you read, pay attention to the setup of the
passage—how it first shows who Christ is and then who we should be in
light of who He is. What words stand out to you? What's the correlation
between this passage and Matthew 5:13–16?

likeminded - same love, one spirit one mind.
exalt Him - tongue acknowledge
do everything w/o grumbling-then you
will shine like the stars in the sky.

In Philippians 2:12–15, Paul says,

Therefore, my dear friends, just as you have always obeyed, so
now, not only in my presence but even more in my absence,
work out your own salvation with fear and trembling. For it is
God who is working in you both to will and to work according
to his good purpose. Do everything without grumbling and arguing, so that you may be blameless and pure, children of God
who are faultless in a crooked and perverted generation, among
whom you shine like stars in the world.

we should be thankful to grow older because so many do not have that opportunity.

Paul admonishes us to work out our salvation—not in order to be saved, since we are saved by grace alone (Eph. 2:8–9), but to live out what God started in us when we first believed. We may have been taught earlier in our faith that we believe in Jesus as our Lord and Savior so we can live with Him forever. And though it is true that salvation leads to a future eternal life, that future eternal life should inform our present life. This means that we practice our faith here and now. Like exercising a muscle in order for it to become stronger, we work out our faith, engaging together with God in the redeeming work He has started in us and in the world until Jesus returns. Our faith should have an impact in this lifetime as "salt of the earth" and "stars in the world."

Just as God created all living things and called them good (Gen. 1), He created us just as we are and called every part of us good. In fact, He calls us *very* good (v. 31). We don't need to hide or exclude any part of ourselves from His purposes, because God desires to show Himself through our lives, our stories, and our beings.

Read Psalm 139:14 from the New International Version, and then write it here in your own words. List every part of you that has been "fearfully and wonderfully made." If there are areas of your life, of yourself, that you've deemed less-than, relabel them now as fearfully and wonderfully made. For example, *My almond-shaped eyes have been fearfully and wonderfully made. My ability to see those on the fringes has been fearfully and wonderfully made.*

Our sufferings can also be used as we are wonderfully made.

My mind is fearfully & wonderfully made. My desire for sugar - was set so I can see your power to override the addiction. You have created me to use my mind to substitute sugar for natural foods. You have challenge me to "change the channel" to other choices that are helpful.

17

Learning to reclaim every part of ourselves as "very good" can be painful as we remember the hurtful words and actions that might have been said or done to us. As you practice this act of reclamation, how does it require you to be courageous?

to be thoughtful. Kind, may my words be sweet. To focus on the specifics, details, to take it all in and not skimp.

Reflect on this prayer and make it your own today:

God, thank You for creating me as I am, for the stories I've lived so far, and for the path You have me on now. Thank You that You desire to impact others through my life and that I don't have to hide or dismiss parts of myself for You to do so. Amen.

Instead, God has chosen what is foolish in the world to shame the wise, and God has chosen what is weak in the world to shame the strong. God has chosen what is insignificant and despised in the world—what is viewed as nothing—to bring to nothing what is viewed as something, so that no one may boast in his presence. It is from him that you are in Christ Jesus, who became wisdom from God for us—our righteousness, sanctification, and redemption—in order that, as it is written: Let the one who boasts, boast in the LORD.

1 Corinthians 1:27-31

I started blogging in 2006 at a time when I especially missed my mother, who'd passed away the year before. I wanted a space to leave thoughts and images for my children to remember me and our lives together, the way I longed for those words from my mom.

I didn't realize that blogging would be a little like going back to high school at forty years old. In many ways it was amazing—the blogosphere was still a relatively small place with a lot of interaction in the comment boxes. There was a strong sense of community, although many of us didn't use our real or full names and worried about privacy.

Some embraced the label "mom blogger," while others rejected it. Most of us were women in the trenches of motherhood, clicking our keyboards in stolen moments between changing diapers, cleaning messy hands and faces, applying Band-Aids, and (for some of us) homeschooling.

We craved a creative outlet and thrived on this new source of adult interaction.

On the flip side, the blogosphere also felt like a popularity contest, where those with the most shares, comments, and subscribers were the adult equivalent of being homecoming queen, head cheerleader, or student council president. For many, checking our statistics became an unhealthy obsession. (Ask me how I know.)

At some point in the hustle of creating a blogging presence, I realized I had sacrificed living real life for online interaction. Don't get me wrong, I believe online friendships can be real and life-giving. But God didn't create us to build platforms just so we could preen ourselves. He created us to have influence starting in our face-to-face communities.

The hustle for each of us might look different. Perhaps it's climbing the ladder of success at your job, being the sought-after mom who knows all the tricks for handling a toddler, or having more knowledge about current events than others. However we seek to build our reputation, at some point in time, we need to prioritize putting our energy into building a well-grounded life with meaningful friendships first over building a platform.

Once I realized this, I turned toward intentionally and vulnerably investing myself in my immediate circle and found that my words had impact right around me.

I thank God for the opportunity to encourage women I'll never meet through words in books or on screens. But seeking to impact the women around me has blessed me in ways I couldn't foresee: I'm not only a better friend, but I've also become a better writer. My friends are active participants in my life story. They're my audience, and they're my cheering section too.

—DAWN CAMP

How have you felt the pressure to hustle and make something of yourself? How does that kind of striving affect the way you view yourself, whether or not you're successful?

I felt tremendous pressure when I was leading a team of 18 women to create the 3rd JLB cookbook. Was I adequate, leader, communicator, organized. I had to give my full attention.

Building a platform and focusing on strategic growth, branding, and marketing are not bad things in and of themselves. Each of them is necessary to grow a business or an organization, and often all of them are required for success.

However, as people of faith, we should have a different standard for how we define success when it comes to our influence and the way we go about gaining it. What does it mean to God and His kingdom to have thousands of followers on social media, to have the ears of hungry women wanting to feed on our content, to have "made it" because we've been asked to speak at conferences or publish books? Does that sort of fame equal more meaningful impact or more glory for God?

To much is given, much is required.

It might seem like it, but when that kind of success becomes the driving force for the way we live, work, and share our lives, it too easily becomes more about ourselves and building our kingdoms instead of God's.

First Corinthians 1:27–31 says that "God has chosen what is *foolish* in the world to shame the wise, and God has chosen what is *weak* in the world to shame the strong. God has chosen what is *insignificant* and *despised* in the world—what is viewed as *nothing*—to bring to nothing what is viewed as something, so that no one may boast in his presence."

We tend to reject what is foolish, weak, insignificant, and despised. And how often have we heard the word *nothing* spoken over us, our gifts, our skills, our lives? Praise God that He sees with divine eyes and considers everything His hands have made as good, as redeemable! Nothing—no one—is useless to the God who chose humanity to be the vessels through whom He would proclaim His saving truth.

What have you considered foolish, weak, or insignificant in your life? Write down a time when God used those very things you considered "nothing" to show Himself to someone.

When on a trip, I made friends with a group of people. I didn't think I'd ever see them again. A year later, I bumped into them in NYC.

Read Joshua 2:1–13. How is Rahab an example of someone who might've been considered "insignificant and despised" but whom God used to make a way for His people?

she was simple, but God "revealed" how he needed her for His purposes.

Rahab was a prostitute who lived in Jericho, the first city the Israelites encountered after coming into the promised land. When Joshua sent spies to survey the land, they ended up at her house, where she hid them and then gave the king's search party wrong directions when they came looking for them. She saved the spies from being discovered, and her act of faith is commended in Hebrews 11, where she's listed among the so-called heroes of faith, including Abraham, Isaac, and Joseph.

God is not bound by human wisdom. He alone chooses who will accomplish His work here on earth.

That means being still (handwritten)

We don't need to hustle for greatness or worth. When we're right where God wants us to be, He can change the course of history through our obedience to Him.

> **When we're right where God wants us to be, He can change the course of history through our obedience to Him.**

In view of God's countercultural requirements for influence, in what areas of your life have you perhaps invested too much time and effort that don't ultimately carry weight in impacting others for God's kingdom?

Sonya Stallings: Every opp in every child's — your child's life is your ministry. (handwritten)

God can use you wherever you are to His glory.

Online Shopping — Realistalking — Social Media — (handwritten)

When we recognize (and really believe) that having influence is not about how much clout we have with others or our status in society or whom we know, we will see that our responsibility is to influence others in a way that shows them who Jesus is. We don't need permission from someone up top (whoever that might be for you) telling us that we can impact others. We are in the communities and families with whom God has placed us, with the friends and neighbors we have, in the job and city we live in, to have influence right where we are.

Write out 1 Corinthians 1:27–31. Read over it three times, paying attention to the words that stick out to you. Write down those words here.

foolish/wise weak/strong despised/popular = nullify

BC of Jesus who has become WISDOM, RIGHTEOUS, HOLY, REDEMPTION —

Boast of Christ — The only way we can boast. (handwritten)

_____

_____

If you've hustled too long after what our world says we should do to
influence others, what's one courageous step you can take to walk away
from that kind of striving? Who is right in front of you or around you that
you could share the truth and love of Jesus with?

We don't have to be as Billy Graham ~~is~~ to share
the gospel. We can go to grocery ∴ share
with the person puts infront of us

_____

The One
thing you
can't
do in
Heaven.
Mark Cayhill

Reflect on this prayer and make it your own today:

_Lord, thank You for showing me through the stories in the Bible
that You are not limited by my humanness. Instead, You choose
to shine through my imperfections, unfazed that that's not how
the world sees greatness. I want to stop striving after inconse-
quential goals, so help me to see where I need to pivot in order
to be in line with where You want me to have influence. Amen._

Jesus said, "Everyone who drinks from this water will
get thirsty again. But whoever drinks from the water
that I will give him will never get thirsty again. In fact,
the water I will give him will become a well of water
springing up in him for eternal life."

"Sir," the woman said to him, "give me this water so
that I won't get thirsty and come here to draw water."

John 4:13–15

Hey, are you going to the baptism service after church?"

My friend asked me this in the middle of my toddler's meltdown. Eyes flashing and jaw set, I'm sure I looked less than approachable, but he still asked.

"I don't know for sure yet," I told him. Obviously, it would depend on making it through the next couple of hours with a cranky toddler (and, admittedly, a cranky mom).

"Okay, well . . ." My friend hesitated, and I realized he was asking for a reason, not simply to be friendly. As it turned out, his son was getting baptized that day, and he wanted me to be there.

For the past couple of years, I'd volunteered with a group of middle school students at our church. Reluctant at first, I quickly fell in love with those kids and looked forward to our time together. Quick to dismiss my influence on them, though, I never considered I was doing actual ministry. I "just" hung out with these kids and tried to walk the thin line between being a cool grown-up friend and a good example.

"Real" ministry was left to the youth director and small group leaders. They were trained. They knew what they were doing. They were important. (Or so I told myself.)

That Sunday morning, though, my friend's son stood in front of our church family and shared his testimony. He talked about how his parents had shown him what it meant to live for God. And then he talked about how I had listened to him and prayed for him months earlier when his family suffered a serious house fire. He named me in his short list of people who'd led him to faith in Jesus!

I was shocked! I burst into tears, and my chest hurt from all the emotions swirling inside. What sticks with me today are gratitude and a deeper understanding of who I am and who Jesus is. No longer can I say that I wasn't doing real ministry; no longer can I say that my time with those kids didn't matter.

From that moment on, I couldn't deny that God was using me to do kingdom work. He didn't need me to be trained or to serve full-time; He wasn't swayed by my previous disinterest in working with kids. He simply needed me to follow Him, and so I did.

—MARY CARVER

How has God chosen to use you even when you didn't consider yourself important or qualified enough?

First time I took a college girl to share our faith, and the girl we shared with, prayed to recieve Christ. Not long after college, she died of a blood disease.

It's easy to diminish the power of our presence when we feel underqualified, but we can never underestimate the way God will move through us by His Spirit.

In the story of the Samaritan woman at the well, Jesus breaks cultural boundaries by talking with her. At that time, rabbis were not supposed to talk with women in public, plus Jews and Samaritans had a long history of religious and ethnic hatred toward one another. Still, Jesus makes His way to Samaria and initiates a conversation with this woman. He shows Himself to be the Messiah by revealing the intimate details about her life. He does this not to condemn her but to bring her toward freedom and restoration.

The Samaritan woman is the kind of person others look down on, a woman who is ostracized from her community. She isn't a qualified or educated religious leader, yet Jesus chooses her to carry the good news about Himself to her whole town. Transformed by her encounter with Him, she becomes a messenger of truth, hope, and redemption, and many believe in Jesus because of her.

Read John 4:7–30. Imagine yourself in the Samaritan woman's place. What is God saying to you through this story?

Go tell everyone : that Christ is the Messiah : He lives and because of that, we live! She wasn't qualified, trained, or educated but her story was used to bring others to Christ.

The Samaritan woman is just one example of how Jesus went about the business of upending cultural norms and expectations—especially regarding those whom society considered less-than, like women and children. He did the same with people who were considered unclean, like lepers and the sick, and with those who were dismissed, like tax collectors, the Samaritans, the poor. He challenged the idea of who was considered worthy of spreading the seeds of the gospel, and most of the time it was not the religious leaders. At key moments in His life, it was women who were present, supportive, chosen. For His birth, Mary was the favored one (Luke 1:26–38). Throughout His ministry, women financially supported His work (Luke 8:2–3). When He was dying, women were at the foot of the cross (John 19:25). And at His resurrection, Mary Magdalene was given the privilege of preaching the good news to the disciples (John 20:11–18).

Jesus brought glory to Himself through the man born blind (John 9:1–41). He scolded the disciples but welcomed little children and blessed them (Luke 18:15–17). And He even noticed Zacchaeus, a despised tax collector, and called out that He wanted to have dinner at his house (Luke 19:1–10).

None of these people were qualified by any worldly or religious standards—not then and not now—yet they were chosen by Jesus.

Education, status, and position are beneficial things, but they are not the only platforms for having influence.

Reflect on your particular location, family, community, city, church, socioeconomic status, and place in other people's lives. How have you seen God move in these areas of your life recently?

Moved to a new home: seen God provide ministry, service, spiritual growth, relationships.

When we think about being women of courageous influence, it's easy to turn our thoughts to all the resources available to us on the internet and all the knowledge we have access to. But from what we've seen of Jesus, perhaps we shouldn't be so concerned with all that. If Jesus chose uneducated, working-class men to be His disciples, the

Samaritan woman to be His evangelist, and a little boy whose lunch fed thousands, imagine what He can do through you and me.

In Christ, we are all considered worthy of carrying the good news, no matter our background, our situation, or our familiarity with church lingo. The good news *has* to be good news for all who hear it—for the poor, the uneducated, those in rural areas and inner cities, the single moms, the lonely, and those living paycheck to paycheck. And who better to carry it, to tell the story of Jesus's redemptive power, than those of us who have experienced it?

> **In Christ, we are all considered worthy of carrying the good news, no matter our background, our situation, or our familiarity with church lingo.**

Let's not disqualify ourselves when God has qualified us with His righteousness as worthy bearers of good news.

In what areas of your life do you feel unqualified to share with others about Jesus? How does knowing that you are chosen by God give you the courage to do so?

In Highschool, I did not know how to voice my faith. NOW, I don't get caught up on words but rather to love others.

Reflect on this prayer and make it your own today:

Lord, thank You for the ways Jesus upended the cultural and religious norms of His day. It gives me a vision and hope for how I can follow in His footsteps and not disqualify myself or others based on outward pedigrees. Help me when I don't have the confidence and when I want to discount myself from the work You are calling me to do. Amen.

Peter turned around and saw behind them the disciple Jesus loved—the one who had leaned over to Jesus during supper and asked, "LORD, who will betray you?" Peter asked Jesus, "What about him, LORD?"

Jesus replied, "If I want him to remain alive until I return, what is that to you? As for you, follow me."

John 21:20-22 NLT

I t was the first writers retreat I'd ever gone to. Instead of breathing in the warm air with gratitude, I felt queasy. Leading up to the retreat, I'd been looking forward to spending time with some people I'd long admired. But as soon as my feet hit the airport floor, I felt sick.

I got to the hotel and saw them: dozens of women I highly esteemed. They were all authors. Some of their books were national and even international bestsellers.

Immediately, a thought slammed itself into my brain: *I don't belong here.*

I shook my head, but the thought didn't go away. Heat spread across my face and neck. I was sure my skin was blotchy.

How could I possibly belong? My résumé held nothing but a part-time Starbucks job and some volunteer work. And sure, my blog had a few readers, but that was mostly my mom and a few of her friends from Bible study.

I stared at the women. I had followed most of them on Instagram for years, and to see them in person instead of as pixels on a screen felt strange and intimidating.

✗ "How could you make me come here, God?" I prayed angrily. The opportunity I once praised and thanked Him for now felt cruel.

I spent most of the three-day retreat alone in my room, licking my wounds. I felt left out and hurt by both God and those writers. I didn't take any responsibility for my feelings. Instead, I kept listening to the same thought loop through my brain:

I don't belong here. I don't belong here. I don't belong here.

I couldn't see the invitation God was extending toward me—an invitation to get to know good, kind, talented women on a deeper level. I missed moments of potential mentorship and moments of human connection. All I could see was my fear and my comparison.

I went home, but instead of giving up, I kept writing and chose to listen to the still, small voice of God.

The next time I was invited to a writers retreat, I decided to show up fully. I brought my whole self, ready to engage in the invitation God was giving me. Instead of feeling envious, I simply felt seen.

I might've allowed comparison to steal from me before, but I never want it to steal from me again.

—ALIZA LATTA

Has there been a time in your life when you felt crippled by comparing yourself with someone else? What ended up happening as a result?

I never felt appropriate next to the Chairman's wife. I always felt childish, underdressed, fake. She always was HIGH UP! Later....my presense made her pace, grab a glass of wine, tremble, embarrassed.

Today's passage highlights Peter, one of Jesus's closest friends and disciples. The combination of his zealousness and humanness holds the door open wide for us to find ourselves in his story.

At the Last Supper, before Jesus is arrested and killed, Peter declares his devotion to Jesus by saying, "I'm ready to die for you" (John 13:37 NLT). Peter's prematurely strong words are dismantled only hours after he speaks them, for that same night he denies the Lord three times, just as Jesus predicted.

In John 21, after Jesus has risen from the dead, He meets His disciples on the seashore. He feeds them breakfast, and then Jesus asks Peter, "Simon, son of John, do you love me more than these?" (v. 15). In this way He intentionally exposes Peter's desire to prove himself better than the others. Three times Jesus asks Peter, "Do you love me?" matching the three times Peter had denied Him. Hurt and humbled, Peter replies three times, "Lord, you know that I love you."

Through this tender moment, Jesus restores the broken relationship Peter had with Him. But no sooner does that happen when Peter notices John following behind them. He asks Jesus, "What about him?" (v. 21).

Perhaps Jesus's words to Peter are what we need to hear today: "What is that to you? As for you, follow me" (v. 22).

When we start comparing ourselves with others—desiring to be like them, envying what they have, trying to run in their lane—we get lost. We trip over ourselves and others, and we lose sight of what we were first called to.

You aren't alone in your struggle. Listen to what God is saying to you: "As for you, follow me."

Where have you most felt the pull to compare yourself with others in your life (e.g., on social media, in friendships, at work, with church acquaintances, with random strangers)?

Am I old? Am I dated? Am I hip? Am I approprate? (Dance Club) Am I plain?

Is there a consistent theme of what triggers comparison in you? If so, can you name it?

appropriate - paying attention - caught up?
Educated vs uneducated. in the word

We often struggle with comparison when we see others get something we want. Maybe someone got the promotion you wanted and even deserved. Maybe a friend announced her surprise pregnancy while you're left wondering when it'll happen for you. Maybe someone has skills you wish you had.

So how do we deal with comparison when it comes up? What truths do we need to recite over ourselves when we start to feel insecure?

First, we need to reestablish our identity. Comparison worms its way deep into our hearts and asks why: *Why am I not there yet? Why is that person getting what I deserve? Why can't I be as gifted, as wealthy, as stress-free? Why do I seem to get the shorter end of the stick?* In essence, we're asking why we can't be that person or live that person's life instead of our own. This kind of thinking makes us lose our center. Off balance, we fall flat on our face, forgetting the One in whom our identity is found.

When you lose your way and yourself in the thick of comparison, listen to what God's Word says about you:

You are beloved. You were created with love, you are loved, and no one and nothing can separate you from the love of God (Rom. 8:38–39).

[handwritten margin notes:]
Truths over comparison
Why) ① Comparing
Result of thinkin' thinkin' we lose our center.
① Beloved.

You are whole even when you feel lacking. God is the one who heals your wounds, fills your emptiness, and meets every single need (Phil. 4:19).

 You have gifts, talents, and a purpose. You were created to love God and others and therefore to become like Christ. Who you are is exactly how God wants to reflect Himself through you (Matt. 5:13–16).

God plugs your holes that make you feel lacking.

Who you are is exactly how God wants to reflect Himself through you.

② Second, we need to know our lane and stay in it. We do this by knowing ourselves and where God has placed us in each season of life. It may not be what you had dreamed of, and it won't be forever, but stay faithful and tethered to Him. He sees the road ahead, and He promises to be with you all the way.

Be where your feet are. Stay in your lane

To release comparison's grip on us, we need to say it out loud and repent if there's envy or bitterness in our hearts. If you're struggling with comparison, write it out in prayer. Tell God all your feelings, what you're desiring, what's stirring in you. Ask God to help you face it.

When comparison starts to creep into your heart, try to stop your thoughts from circling around the drain of despair, acknowledge to yourself that you're disappointed or mad or jealous, and then recognize that another person's good news or success doesn't change who you are or whose you are.

It's okay if your disappointment stays for a while. Take some deep, grounding breaths and reestablish your identity as we talked about before.

**Read Romans 8:38–39, Philippians 4:19, and Matthew 5:13–16.
Record what words or verses stand out to you as you consider your
struggle with comparison.**

Nothing can separate me from God's ♡.
He will meet all of my needs according to His riches.
A light of a Hill can not be hidden - glorify
·your heaven is show good deeds to glorify Him.
    Father

Reflect on this prayer and make it your own today:

*Father, it's so hard not to compare myself with others, whether
it's my physical body, status, situation, talents, or resources.
The pull to compare is everywhere. Whenever I face the struggle
to compare, bring to mind the truths about my identity. Anchor
me when I feel despondent, and help me to find my confidence in
You. Amen.*

Gratitude is the antithesis of comparison.

But you are not like that, for you are a chosen people. You are royal priests, a holy nation, God's very own possession. As a result, you can show others the goodness of God, for he called you out of the darkness into his wonderful light.

1 Peter 2:9 NLT

I knew from the moment we received my husband's stage 4 cancer diagnosis that God intended to use our story for His glory. God made me a storyteller, a messenger. He prepared me in advance for this work and gave me gifts for writing and speaking. For years God had been using mentors and friends to speak this truth over me. I had countless conversations, listened to sermons, and heard messages at conferences that resonated this same idea.

The question was, would I be willing to believe in my worth as a woman of influence and do what God was calling me to do—to share my story of grief and glory?

At first I resisted. I didn't want to be known as the "grief lady." I didn't want to be vulnerable and share my pain publicly. Four months after my husband soared to heaven, I began to write. I immediately started to outline a Bible study about looking for God's glory in the middle of grief. This was my personal story, but it was also an invitation for women to learn how to chase after God's glory in their own trials.

Each week I wrote a chapter of what would eventually become a Bible study called *Glory Chasers: Discovering God's Glory in Unexpected Places*. I invited nine of my closest friends to meet with me and go through the study. God used this sweet time of fellowship to heal us as we traversed through grief and loss together.

That fall, my church invited me to teach the *Glory Chasers* study for a group of over two hundred women. Though I didn't feel ready, God began using my personal testimony of how He was present with me through the suffering and grief to challenge and encourage a larger audience, and by the following spring I decided to pursue publication. The more I saw God working through my words, the more I knew I couldn't keep the message to myself.

God has written and continues to write His story in each of us, and whether you share yours on a stage before many or with a friend via text, God wants to do it through *you*—your words, your voice, your experiences.

Now people know me as the "glory lady" instead of the "grief lady." Every time I share this message, God reminds me that He chose me to lead, to encourage, and to proclaim His glory as I chase after Him in my own life.

—DORINA LAZO GILMORE-YOUNG

Write about a time when you chose to believe in your worth as a woman of influence and did the thing God was calling you to do.

-begin to write, begin to share at church's
∴ Garden Clubs. Shared at a Wive's Golf
tournament., T.V.

The Warrior is a Child. Twilla Parris.

Old Test

New Test.

In Hebrews 5:1, we read that a high priest is one who represents or acts as the mediator between human beings and God. In the tabernacle and later the temple (the places of worship for the Israelites in biblical history), it was only the high priest who could enter into the Holy of Holies—the innermost place where God's presence dwelled. Once a year the high priest would go in to sprinkle the sacrificial animal's blood and atone for his own sins and the sins of the people.

In the Old Testament, God's people had to obey the law of Moses and rely on the high priest to make sacrifices for their sins. But Jesus changed all that. He fulfilled the law and paid the sacrifice for all humankind. Because of Him, the privilege of ministry has been decentralized from the one to everyone who believes in His name. Thus, we are all able to come fully into God's presence just as we are, with no fear of death or condemnation, because Christ is our most High Priest. And in Him we have the privilege and responsibility of ministering to one another as a priesthood of believers.

How does this understanding of ministering to one another change the way you see yourself as part of the church—whether that's in your local church community or in the global body of Christ (Church with a capital *C*)?

Anyone is capable to minister, pray, share, give testimony,

Though we all have the calling to minister to one another, we often expect only pastors and leaders in the church to teach us, shepherd us, and lead us with divinely anointed knowledge and wisdom.

Jesus alone is the great High Priest for us all, and we are *all* meant to care for one another with our gifts and skills, with a listening ear

Body of Christ

and an empathetic heart. We *all* get to enter into God's presence, hear His voice, and speak His truth over each other. This is what the body of Christ is supposed to look like—each of us functioning fully as ourselves, connected interdependently for the health of the whole body. As Paul reminds us in 1 Corinthians 12,

> But our bodies have many parts, and God has put each part just where he wants it. How strange a body would be if it had only one part! Yes, there are many parts, but only one body. The eye can never say to the hand, "I don't need you." The head can't say to the feet, "I don't need you." . . . All of you together are Christ's body, and each of you is a part of it. (vv. 18–21, 27 NLT)

Read through the spiritual gifts Paul lists in 1 Corinthians 12:8–11, 27–31. Write down the spiritual gifts you have.

wisdom, knowledge, faith in the Spirit.
Work of the Spirit!

This week we've talked about how we were made to shine, that we were made to have influence *because* we have been made new in Christ. Our influence isn't based on what culture says it should be or on our worldly qualifications or lack thereof. God considers everything His hands have made as good, as worthy of carrying His good news.

We are women of influence, period. Let's embrace the way God made us for impact.

Knowing God has placed you where you are and chosen you to have influence with those around you, remember not to look to the right or left, wondering what someone else is doing. Instead, let's be women who stay in our lanes.

"Driving past trucks!"

Let's be faithful to stay on whatever road He has us on. We are women of influence, period. Let's embrace the way God made us for impact.

How does understanding the importance of ministering to one another give you the courage to embrace and use your God-given gifts?

Be sure you can see it, feel it, know it and claim it to share with someone else.

Reflect on this prayer and make it your own today:

Lord, thank You for making me a woman of influence. Thank You that because Jesus is my High Priest, I can minister to others through my spiritual gifts, my talents, and my words. I'm so grateful that You choose to do Your work through me. If I start to lose my way or forget who You made me to be, remind me of what I've learned this week, and may Your grace bring me back to firm ground again. Amen.

not position, but place and a willing yes

If you love me, you will keep my commands.

John 14:15

The handyman showed up on my front porch on a day when I had no margin. Between looming deadlines and a mile-long to-do list, I hoped he would gather what he needed for an estimate and be on his way lickety-split.

The chuckle when he spoke told me otherwise. So did his crinkly laugh lines. Before he even entered our house, he was chattering away, dispensing home remedies for our annoying carpenter bees.

This guy was a character, and I already liked him.

Cheerfully, he explained his process, all the while measuring and making notes. When I finally circled back to determine his availability, our conversation took a very unexpected turn. I learned he had stage 4 cancer.

Somehow he was still smiling. His remarkable attitude dammed up my blubbery eyes.

The more personal details he shared, the faster my heart raced. I sensed God leading me beyond my comfort zone, calling me to simple obedience rooted in love.

Though tempted to send him off with an "I'll pray for you," I knew actually praying with him right then would be completely different. And yet, truthfully, I was equal parts certain and uncertain. Would he think I was some kind of Jesus freak? Might this offend him or make him uncomfortable?

Deep down, I knew this was no time to give in to people-pleasing. The greatest commands are to love God and others, and right in front of me was an opportunity to obey both.

Knowing nothing about his faith and wondering what he'd think, I blurted, "Can I pray for you?"

There was more at stake than my awkward feelings. Here stood a person in need of God. If I believed what Jesus plainly said—"If you love me, you will keep my commands"—then not following the Holy Spirit's leading would be unloving and disobedient.

The man's immediate yes was a gift. I gestured toward our front door, and we walked outside. There, we bowed our heads and prayed at the spot I had met him barely an hour before. I decided in that moment that a Southern front porch is as fine a place as any to come to Jesus.

—ROBIN DANCE

When have you obeyed a nudging or a word from God even when it was out of character or uncomfortable for you?

_____

_____

_____

_____

During the Last Supper with His disciples, Jesus knew it would soon be time for Him to face death. In John 13:1 we're told that "he had loved his disciples during his ministry on earth, and now he loved them to the very end." John goes on to say, "Jesus knew that the Father had given him authority over everything and that he had come from God and would return to God. *So* he got up from the table, took off his robe, wrapped a towel around his waist, and poured water into a basin. Then he began to wash the disciples' feet, drying them with the towel he had around him" (vv. 3–5 NLT).

It's often our everyday encounters and mundane tasks that provide opportunities for both obedience and influence. Robin showed the love of God to a handyman giving her an estimate. Jesus humbly chose a servant's task so that everyone would understand the depth of His love.

> **True love motivates and moves us into action—in other words, obedience.**

True love motivates and moves us into action—in other words, obedience. And when we listen to God's nudges out of love for Him and others, we bring about blessing.

After Jesus washed His disciples' feet, He gave them instructions to do the same, ending with, "Now that you know these things, God will bless you for doing them" (John 13:17 NLT).

Obedience leads to blessing—for us and for others.

Imagine you were a disciple and Jesus washed your feet. What do you learn about God's character and love through Jesus's actions?

Read Philippians 2:5–8. How does humility tie into love and action?

Jesus washing His disciples' feet shows the upside-down way of influencing others. He is God, yet He doesn't stubbornly grasp at His divine identity to prove Himself. He doesn't lord it over His disciples or tell them to wash each other's feet without showing them how. Instead, He bends low, "assuming the form of a servant, taking on the likeness of humanity" (Phil. 2:7). He becomes like them—like us—even willing to be "obedient to the point of death" (v. 8).

Humility must precede obedience if we are to act in accordance with God's love and not simply out of obligation. Influencing others in the way Jesus did means emptying ourselves of any desire to be lifted up or admired for our obedience. When we are sure of our identity in Christ, we can love and serve others without an agenda.

Love for God leads to obedience, which in turn looks like love for others. It's a beautiful cycle, and it often involves saying quiet yeses in response to the Spirit's nudging, as Robin found out.

So what does it look like to sense the Spirit's nudging or to hear God's voice? There are various ways God speaks to His people. In the Bible, we see examples of God speaking through an audible voice, through the sound of thunder, and through the voice of a prophet. Sometimes God spoke to His people through visions or dreams or angels. Other times He spoke through leaders or priests. But one of the most relatable examples is when God spoke to the prophet Elijah in a still, small voice (1 Kings 19:11–13).

When Robin sensed God leading her out of her comfort zone, she knew in her gut that God was prompting her to pray right then and there on her porch. By paying attention to how God was moving in her mind, spirit, and soul in that moment, she was able to recognize what she needed to do.

Listening to those nudges prompted her to pray, and by the handyman's immediate yes, we know his heart was ready to receive. Who knows how he was affected by her prayers and how he might have felt comforted and encouraged by the words she spoke over him?

We may not always see the effects of our influence on others, but we can trust that God will take our small yeses and use them for His purposes.

Each yes we say makes obedience easier the next time around. What is a small yes you can say to God? It could be praying over someone, sending them a text, or sharing an encouraging word with them.

_____

_____

_____

_____

Reflect on this prayer and make it your own today:

God, thank You for calling me Your beloved and that it's from this place of love that You ask me to obey. Thank You for sometimes speaking to me loud and clear and other times through Your still, small voice. When it's hard to know what I should do, help me and confirm Your word to me. And even when I'm not sure, I pray that I can step out in faith and do what You're asking. Increase my faith. Amen.

The king of Aram had great admiration for Naaman, the commander of his army, because through him the LORD had given Aram great victories. But though Naaman was a mighty warrior, he suffered from leprosy.

At this time Aramean raiders had invaded the land of Israel, and among their captives was a young girl who had been given to Naaman's wife as a maid. One day the girl said to her mistress, "I wish my master would go to see the prophet in Samaria. He would heal him of his leprosy."

2 Kings 5:1–3 NLT

A few years ago, I compiled a book on marriage and enlisted the assistance of eight friends. They agreed to brainstorm discussion questions and help me write a study guide before the book's release. I distributed spiral-bound copies my publisher sent us and made reservations for a table at Starbucks, where we met five times over a three-week period.

Most of the women were in their thirties and forties, while the youngest was in her early twenties and had been married less than a year. Those of us who had been wed for a decade or two were amazed at how well our youngest member could gather our disjointed ideas and craft thought-provoking questions.

In the beginning, each of these women knew me and at least one of the others, but they weren't all friends. After weeks of working our way through topic categories like "As Long as We Both Shall Live," "For

Better or for Worse," and "The Refining Power of Marriage," even those who'd never met before the study came to know each other on a fairly intimate level.

I loved watching my worlds merge as these friendships grew week by week. When the guide was finished, we culminated our time together with a celebration at a restaurant with our husbands. And just like the wives, these men became fast friends too.

We set out to create a study guide that would impact the lives of readers, providing encouragement to both the newlywed and the woman celebrating her golden anniversary. We had no idea that our time together would impact our own lives, not just for that season but for years to come.

No doubt it's easier to dwell within our established friend circles—it's more comfortable and secure. But whenever I see this group of women interacting on social media or in person, it fills me with joy and gratefulness that I had the opportunity to bring them together in a way that forged deeper bonds and new, meaningful friendships.

—DAWN CAMP

When did a small thing you said or did have a greater impact than you imagined?

In 2 Kings 5:1–19, we meet Naaman, a commander of the Aramean army (modern-day Syria). He is a mighty warrior, highly esteemed by his king, but he suffers from leprosy—a disease we now understand could have ranged from superficial skin issues to major deformities. Though it's not certain how severe Naaman's condition is, we can infer from the text that he is eager to be healed from it.

And this is where we meet the girl who changes his life.

The Arameans had invaded Israel and taken some of its people captive. One of them was a young girl who was given to Naaman's wife as a slave. The young girl says to her mistress one day, "I *wish* my master would go to see the prophet in Samaria. He would heal him of his leprosy" (5:3 NLT). In other translations like the CSB and NIV, she says, "*If only* my master would see the prophet in Samaria!"

The potential for healing was embedded in this girl's words, and that's all Naaman needs to start his journey for a cure.

With permission from the king, Naaman goes to Israel to find the prophet Elisha, whom the girl had told him about. Elisha instructs Naaman to wash in the Jordan River seven times to be healed—a baptism of sorts. In the Bible, the number seven represents wholeness or perfection, and baptism represents the transformation from death to life. Even Jesus Himself was baptized in the Jordan River before He went into the wilderness prior to starting His ministry.

Naaman eventually obeys, submerging himself seven times, and he comes out with his skin restored "as healthy as the skin of a young child" (5:14 NLT).

Death to life. Sickness to wholeness.

Because this girl who had been stolen from her people and her land spoke up, Naaman is not only physically healed but also has a spiritual renewal: "From now on I will never again offer burnt offerings or sacrifices to any other god except the LORD" (5:17 NLT).

> **Using our influence for the sake of others takes courage, but lives will be changed through it.**

Using our influence for the sake of others takes courage, but lives will be changed through it—whether it's speaking a simple word of encouragement to a stranger, creating space for people to connect with one another, or going out of our way to help someone experience God.

Wherever you find yourself—in pleasant or difficult or surprising circumstances—God is at work. How can you be courageous in using your influence for the people around you?

The phrase "It's who you know" demonstrates the impact of your personal connections and the power of word of mouth. Our lives are interwoven in ways that are both miraculous and mysterious, not by chance but by grace. And in our relationships with others, we have the opportunity to wield our words to tear down or to build up, to harm or to heal.

Proverbs 15:23 says, "Everyone enjoys a fitting reply; it is wonderful to say the right thing at the right time!" (NLT).

The influence we have in someone's life often comes down to our words—which ones we use, the timing of them, the tone we have. It might be an invitation to join a discussion group, like in Dawn's story. It might be an "I see you" when someone shares their marital strife or a quiet "I love you" to a friend who just lost a parent to cancer.

To say the right thing at the right time, we need help from the Holy Spirit and eyes to see how He might be moving in a person's life. We need to pay attention to where He's placed us and whom we're with, and we must have courage to speak when it is time.

Is there a specific situation in your life right now in which it *is* the right time for you to speak up? Write down the person who needs to hear what you need to say, then pray for the right timing.

The Israelite girl from Naaman's story was living in a situation she didn't ask for, in a country that wasn't her own, with no power to change her circumstances. There will be times when we won't have control over our lives, when we might feel helpless or hopeless, but even in those times, God is still there.

God's presence cannot be shut out; His power cannot be made weak. He leans His ear to His children when they cry out, and there is no end to His promise of being with us to the end. As Psalm 139:7–12 says,

> Where can I go from your Spirit?
>   Where can I flee from your presence?
> If I go up to the heavens, you are there;
>   if I make my bed in the depths, you are there.
> If I rise on the wings of the dawn,
>   if I settle on the far side of the sea,
> even there your hand will guide me,
>   your right hand will hold me fast.
> If I say, "Surely the darkness will hide me
>   and the light become night around me,"
> even the darkness will not be dark to you;
>   the night will shine like the day,
>   for darkness is as light to you. (NIV)

Even in the most desperate places, God is speaking and moving. No one is beyond His healing hand, and you may be just the person through whom that healing comes.

Whether or not you're in difficult circumstances, how does God's presence give you the courage to wield your influence for the good and life of those around you?

Reflect on this prayer and make it your own today:

God, thank You for being present in difficult circumstances and for wanting to bring healing through me. Give me wisdom to speak the right words at the right time and to be a source of hope—even for those I might consider my enemies. Help me to see how I can use my influence to create spaces for others to experience Your presence. Amen.

The angel replied to her, "The Holy Spirit will come upon you, and the power of the Most High will overshadow you. Therefore, the holy one to be born will be called the Son of God. And consider your relative Elizabeth—even she has conceived a son in her old age, and this is the sixth month for her who was called childless. For nothing will be impossible with God."

"See, I am the LORD's servant," said Mary. "May it happen to me as you have said." Then the angel left her.

Luke 1:35–38

Ages ago, my husband and I lived and worked at a Bible camp on the prairie of North Dakota. While we were in a wilderness place physically, we were also in one emotionally. We were far from our families, lonelier than we had ever been, and we had been trying to have a baby for more than three years. One day, after such a long wait and struggle, there were two pink lines and one huge celebration. But soon after that, I had a miscarriage, and it was the worst day of my life.

That wilderness season brought me to my knees, seeking comfort and peace. God whispered that I wasn't alone in my pain, and I believed Him. So I started writing the honest, behind-the-scenes stories of my heart in the only venue available to me—the internet. My heart was willing to share about our infertility and loss, and I hoped to find kindred souls somewhere out there.

I turned my blog, which I'd originally started to keep our family and friends posted on camp life, into a processing place for my heart. I shared about the loneliness. I shared about our infertility struggle. I shared the joy when we were expecting, and I shared the pain when that dream crumbled around us. I wrote willingly, offering my story up in faith, never knowing where it might land, but knowing it helped my own heart at the very least.

Ultimately, God called us out of that wilderness season. We moved, we got new jobs and a new home, and after another devastating pregnancy loss, we eventually had four children. We returned to a beloved church, and one spring Sunday a dear woman in her seventies approached me in the parking lot. She thanked me for my blog posts and confessed she had never shared her own experience of pregnancy loss but was able to do so with me that day. She told me she felt unburdened by simply telling her story, and she would hold it in no longer.

It wasn't the first time I'd been told that very thing: "I've never talked about this before . . ." But then they would begin. And tearfully, we would honor a life that was.

I had no pull with these women as a social influencer, no platform or reach to boast of. I simply wrote my story with a willing heart, and others were moved to tell theirs.

—ANNA RENDELL

The key idea in Anna's story is that she was willing. How is trusting God connected to being willing to use your influence for Him?

In Luke 1, the angel Gabriel visits Zechariah, the future father of John the Baptist, and Mary, the future mother of Jesus. Both are told they will have a child, and both babies will be miracles.

Gabriel tells Zechariah that the Lord has heard his cry and that his wife, Elizabeth, will have a baby even though she has been barren and they are both old. This baby boy is to be named John and will one day become a prophet to turn people's hearts toward God.

Zechariah responds, "How can I know this? For I am an old man, and my wife is well along in years" (Luke 1:18).

Zechariah doubts how this could happen without proof of possibility. He doesn't have the faith to believe what he cannot see, and because of his disbelief God causes him to be mute until his son is born.

On the other hand, when Gabriel approaches Mary to tell her she will bear a son, she responds by saying, "How can this be, since I have not had sexual relations with a man?" (Luke 1:34).

Though Mary's answer sounds similar to Zechariah's, her response is less about doubt and more about curiosity.

When the angel explains that the Holy Spirit will overshadow her and that nothing is impossible with God, Mary answers, "See, I am the Lord's servant. May it happen to me as you have said" (Luke 1:38).

Mary receives the words spoken over her without reluctance, and her willingness to embrace God's plan shows that she trusts the One who chose her.

How does God's trustworthiness help with your willingness to influence others as He asks of you?

_____

_____

_____

_____

Have you ever received a clear direction from God but struggled with doubt? What made it hard for you to trust God's word or plan?

_____

_____

_____

_____

God's plan for Mary and Zechariah didn't come with long-term instructions, and for many of us, trusting someone's word without knowing concrete plans feels reckless and foolish. Yet isn't that what faith is? Hebrews 11:1 says, "Now faith is the reality of what is hoped for, the proof of what is not seen." Faith, by definition, is trusting a reality that we cannot see. And obedience in faith usually means we take the step to obey even when we can't see where our foot will land.

> **Obedience in faith usually means we take the step to obey even when we can't see where our foot will land.**

Faith is the pathway to being willing, knowing that God sees something we cannot.

In Mark 12:41–44 there's a short story about a poor widow who offered everything she had at the temple. Though many rich people gave far more than she did, Jesus tells His disciples that they gave out of a surplus of their wealth, whereas the widow gave everything she had.

She trusted that her offering would please God and that He would provide and care for her afterward. Jesus honors her for her willingness to give "all she had to live on" (v. 44), pointing out that her impact wasn't in her wealth but in her lived-out example of faith.

Is there something that you're holding back from God—possibly a part of yourself or a part of your finances? In what area of your life do you need to practice courageous willingness?

_____

_____

_____

_____

In the story of the poor widow, Jesus points out that it isn't how much money people put into the collection box that matters. What matters more to Him is *where* the offering comes from—the state of their hearts, their motivation.

In 1 Samuel 15 we see an example of what not to do when King Saul offers a sacrifice he wasn't supposed to. He had been commanded by God to completely destroy the nation of Amalek, but he chose to spare the king and the best of the sheep and cattle. Later, he offers the animals in sacrifice to God, thinking it will honor God and justify his disobedience.

Saul doesn't understand that he completely missed the mark until Samuel, Israel's prophet and priest at that time, rebukes him: "Does the Lord take pleasure in burnt offerings and sacrifices as much as in obeying the Lord? Look: to obey is better than sacrifice, to pay attention is better than the fat of rams" (v. 22).

To obey, to pay attention, is better than any sacrifice we can make.

So we don't need to worry that what we have to offer is too small or unworthy. We don't have to bedazzle our offerings or even know all the reasons why God is asking us to do something. Neither Mary nor Zechariah could have understood the scope of what lay ahead for them, but we can do as Mary did. We can have courage to obey.

Reflect on 1 Samuel 15:22 again. What have you offered to God thinking it would please Him instead of just obeying what He asked of you in the first place?

_____

_____

_____

_____

If you feel reluctant to obey God, write down some times when He's proven His trustworthiness to you, and ask Him to give you the courageous willingness to obey.

_____

_____

_____

_____

Reflect on this prayer and make it your own today:

Lord, thank You that You look at the heart and not the quantity of what I bring. I acknowledge that there are days when it's easier to bring You sacrifices You didn't ask for when You really just asked for my obedience. Whether it's because I'm afraid or because I lack trust in You, help me to take a step forward into obedience. I pray for a willing heart so I can respond as Mary did and say, "May it happen to me as you have said." Amen.

Truly I tell you, unless a grain of wheat falls to the ground and dies, it remains by itself. But if it dies, it produces much fruit.

John 12:24

The day I gave my two weeks' notice was a roller coaster of emotion. I felt ecstatic to escape a job and a company I disliked. I felt sad to leave a couple of coworkers behind. I felt frustrated that the potential this job had held three years earlier never quite materialized. And I felt scared that I was giving up not just my dreams but my identity.

I had thought by that point in life I'd be a success—someone others would recognize as having "made it." But well into my thirties, I found myself stuck in an entry-level position, and no matter how many résumés I sent or interviews I had, I couldn't find a way up or out. At the same time my husband and I were juggling childcare and struggling with his hours at work. My family needed me at home even as employers didn't seem to need me at all. It seemed like I didn't have a choice but to quit my full-time job—and my job search—to stay home with my daughter.

I ended up never returning to the career I left or the workaholic ways I'd developed, though I did start working part-time about a year later. I miss that old life sometimes. But what I miss more than the specific work is the potential for the kind of success I once longed for— success that could be measured, that had a clear-cut path to determine achievement, that would be admired when people asked me, "So what do you do?"

I had to let my dreams of success die in order to have open hands for the new dreams God was starting in me. Instead of a corporate job, I said yes to pursuing writing. Out of what felt like the death of my desires came the opportunity to spend more time with my family and serve God through ministries I couldn't have been a part of if I had continued striving for promotions and recognition.

I'll admit that even as I stay faithful to this life God has given me, every now and then I feel the sting of losing that other life. But even though I may not be successful by the world's standards, I stand assured that I'm more like the woman God created me to be—one who looks more like Jesus.

—MARY CARVER

Have you ever experienced the death of your dreams? What were those dreams, and how did it feel to have them end?

As Mary discovered, staying in step with God's plan isn't always easy, but it does lead to a meaningful life. No one knew this better than Jesus, as we see in John 12.

Jesus came to Jerusalem for the Passover festival. He entered the city on a donkey's colt while the crowds waved palm branches and shouted, "Hosanna! Blessed is he who comes in the name of the Lord—the King of Israel!" (v. 13). They had seen Him raise Lazarus from the dead, and they were hoping He would lead them into political freedom from Roman rule. But their desire for what they wanted Jesus to be was not His dream for them.

His dream was for the redemption of all things, for freedom from sin, and for a restored relationship with God. But it came at a cost.

Jesus said in John 12:24, "Truly I tell you, unless a grain of wheat falls to the ground and dies, it remains by itself. But if it dies, it produces much fruit." The seed must die in order to bear fruit—meaning Jesus had to die in order for all of them (and all of us) to have life as well.

This was the fulfillment of what the original Passover was about, as we find in the Old Testament book of Exodus.

When the Israelites were about to be delivered from slavery in Egypt, God gave them instructions about what each household must do to prepare for the exodus. A lamb or young goat was to be sacrificed and its blood smeared on the wooden door frames of their houses. As the angel of death went throughout Egypt in the night and killed all the firstborn (the last of the ten plagues), the blood was a sign to pass over that house and spare the lives of those inside.

Jesus offered Himself as the once-for-all Passover Lamb, and His blood smeared the wooden cross where He hung. He is the Seed that died so fruit could be born.

Death before life is the way of Jesus, and so it is the pattern for our life in Him as well.

How have you seen this death-to-life pattern in your life or in the lives of those around you?

A baby being born is a great example of a death-to-life pattern. Read John 3:1–17. What do you think it means to be born again?

_____

_____

_____

_____

Nicodemus, a Pharisee, comes to see Jesus after dark, wanting to understand more about Him. Jesus tells him that unless he is born again, he cannot see the kingdom of God.

When a baby emerges from her mother's womb, she begins a completely different life than she has known thus far. The baby leaves the darkness of the womb and enters light. Her eyes are opened. She breathes and eats in new ways. She interacts with others and becomes an integral part of her community. Her life exists because her mother gave of herself—in essence, died to herself.

Being women of God will require us to experience this process of dying in order for life to be brought forth through us—particularly as we seek to use our influence to bring others into the light.

As you reflect on these metaphors of new birth and life after death, what is God saying to you about the "deaths" you are facing now?

_____

_____

_____

_____

Perhaps you're in the thick of the dying process, and you feel disoriented and full of despair. It could be that you're facing the loss of a loved one and the overwhelming decisions that need to be made. It could be the end of lifelong dreams you had hoped and planned for or the unexpected end of a marriage. It could be the loss of community from a cross-country move or the loss of reputation from unjust gossip. And then there are the many deaths we experience as our flesh—our old way of being—dies: death to our selfishness, our need for control, our addictions, our apathy, our prejudice.

The dying process is always painful, but death is not the end of the story. Jesus rode into Jerusalem that day facing His crucifixion. He suffered and died and stayed dead for three days, but still the story continued. He rose from the grave and confirmed the new narrative we have in Him—that with every death, the hope of life is always present.

It doesn't mean life in Christ is easy and beautiful all the time. It's quite the opposite. Every time we choose to be like Christ instead of defaulting to our old way of being, it will feel like death. But we will know Christ more. As Paul says in Philippians 3:7–8, "But whatever were gains to me I now consider loss for the sake of Christ. What is more, I consider everything a loss because of the surpassing worth of knowing Christ Jesus my Lord, for whose sake I have lost all things. I consider them garbage, that I may gain Christ" (NIV).

> **No matter how painful or dreadful death can be, we have a God who understands how it feels, stays with us when it's dark, and guides us like a mother into the light.**

No matter how painful or dreadful death can be, we have a God who understands how it feels, stays with us when it's dark, and guides us like a mother into the light. Everything dims in comparison with the reward of Christ.

Write out John 3:16 and 12:24, and write down the connections of death to life you see between them.

Reflect on this prayer and make it your own today:

God, thank You that Your story didn't end with death. Thank You for the hope of life even in the process of dying. Help me to have courage to let things die when it's time to let them go in order for me to embrace the life You have for me. Amen.

And the angel came to her and said, "Greetings, favored woman! The LORD is with you." But she was deeply troubled by this statement, wondering what kind of greeting this could be. Then the angel told her, "Do not be afraid, Mary, for you have found favor with God."

Luke 1:28–30

I often find inspiration when I'm out running. There's something about the rhythm of steps and the cadence of breath that gives me space to hear from God and create. I set out on the trail near my brother's house in Southern California. As I slipped into a familiar pace, words flooded my heart.

It's not uncommon for writing ideas to bubble up while I run, but this time was different. I couldn't stop composing this particular spoken-word piece for mothers of all kinds. I could hear the sound of the words and phrases harmonizing in my head.

It had been almost two decades since I wrote and shared a spoken-word piece on a stage. In my early twenties I had frequented poetry slams, coffee shop open mics, and events at local museums. When I got married and became a mama, I moved away from that world. My voice found a more comfortable place to land on blogs and in women's Bible studies, school classrooms, MOPS meetings, and conferences.

But sometimes God presses a message into our hearts, and we cannot escape it.

Was it any wonder when I got a call about a month later from the worship and arts pastor at our church? He and our lead pastor had a vision for someone sharing a series of spoken-word pieces in the services leading up to Mother's Day. I hadn't told anyone except my husband what I had been working on. I never would have dreamed my own church would be interested. My heart danced with a swirl of excitement and fear.

What would people think when they heard the sound of my voice? How would they receive a spoken-word piece in church? Should I put this heart-piece out there for all to hear and possibly critique?

Yes.

It was clear that despite my own fears and insecurity, God ordained this opportunity in advance. He chose me for such a time as this. I couldn't question His timing or His method for showing me I was the woman to deliver this specific message. I had to trust Him.

A few weeks later, I found myself standing backstage, hands trembling. Violin, guitar, and vocals filled the air. I stepped into the spotlight and the words flowed. Somehow the fear melted and gave way to courage that could only come from the Holy Spirit.

—DORINA LAZO GILMORE-YOUNG

When was the last time you did something even though you were afraid, because you knew it was God's invitation to you?

We end this week by circling back to the story of Mary, the mother of Jesus. Mary is from Nazareth in Galilee, a poor village that had a negative reputation. She is young, most likely still a teenager, and is engaged to a man named Joseph.

By all outward appearances, Mary is just a regular girl living an ordinary life. We're not told anything about her or her circumstances that would set her apart as special or holy. And yet this is the girl God chooses.

The angel Gabriel appears to her and says, "Greetings, favored woman! The Lord is with you" (Luke 1:28). The word *favored* also means "graced" or "blessed," which is how Mary is later described when she visits her cousin Elizabeth (1:42–45). Mary has God's favor, God's grace, God's blessing on her. She has no outward status or worldly wealth; she is simply chosen by Him. Mary is favored by God to influence the world by bearing the Messiah.

And her response to the angel, as we discussed earlier this week, is one of willingness. Elizabeth, the wife of Zechariah and the mother of John the Baptist, says to her, "You are blessed because you believed that the Lord would do what he said" (Luke 1:45 NLT).

Mary, in contrast to Zechariah, believes what the angel says and receives it without doubt. Her willingness to trust God in this enormous call to bear His Son is evidence of her blessedness.

Look up the following verses and write down the characteristics or qualities of God that make Him trustworthy.

    Psalm 9:10

    Isaiah 25:1

    1 Thessalonians 5:24

All three words—*favored, blessed, graced*—have the implicit requirement of receiving. How does having a posture of open hands relate to being a woman of influence?

After the angel's strange greeting to her, Mary is bewildered. *Me? A favored woman?* But Gabriel reassures her, saying, "Do not be afraid, Mary, for you have found favor with God" (Luke 1:30). This is one of many "do not be afraid" moments in the Bible.

When Joshua takes over leadership of the Israelite nation, Moses tells him, "Do not be afraid or discouraged. For the LORD your God is with you wherever you go" (Josh. 1:9 NLT).

When the disciples are caught in a storm and they see Jesus walking on water toward them, Jesus says, "Don't be afraid. Take courage! I am here!" (Mark 6:50 NLT).

When Jesus is raised back to life, He appears to the women who came to His tomb and says to them, "Don't be afraid!" (Matt. 28:10 NLT).

It's human to be afraid. Fear is a natural response to scary, out-of-control situations or to an unpredictable future. It's what makes us cautious and keeps us in check when we bump up against things that might hurt us.

But when fear is the framework through which we live life, when it paralyzes us and keeps us from moving forward in obedience, our scale of fear and courage has become imbalanced, and we need to be recalibrated.

Each "do not be afraid" command in the Bible is intended not so we will simply get rid of our feelings of fear but so we will have courage in the face of fear.

Gabriel's greeting to Mary is followed by the assurance "The Lord is with you" (Luke 1:28). God's presence is the reason we can say yes to the things He asks of us. He will not leave us on our own but promises to be Immanuel, God with us.

Rewrite the sentence below and fill in the blank with every fear-filled situation you're in. Read the sentences out loud to yourself once you have them all written down.

Do not be afraid when _____, because the Lord is with you.

\

_____

_____

_____

_____

Like Mary, we are called favored women when we have faith to believe God's word to us. Having influence is not about a position we hold or a status we can claim. We can have influence right where God has placed us because this is exactly where He has chosen to do His work through us. We may not be able to see all the reasons why, and we might feel unsure whether we're hearing Him correctly. But all He asks of us is a willing yes.

Dorina understood that God had chosen her for that moment in time to perform her spoken word at her church. She was able to face her fears and insecurity and have courage to take the stage. Loving God means obeying Him, and obeying Him brings blessing to us (because we get to know Him more) and to others (because they get to know Him more). This is the fruit that comes from our obedience. May we be willing to say yes to Him even when we're afraid.

May we be willing to say yes to Him even when we're afraid.

What has God been showing you about Himself through your obedience?

_____

_____

You are a favored, chosen woman. How does that give you courage to do what God is asking of you today?

Reflect on this prayer and make it your own today:

Lord, thank You for the words You spoke over Mary. You called her "favored woman," and I thank You for choosing me as well. When You ask me to do something, I want to be ready and willing to say yes. I trust that You have planted my feet where I am now, and I want to know You and make You known in this place. Amen.

be a person of integrity

Woe to you, scribes and Pharisees, hypocrites! You clean the outside of the cup and dish, but inside they are full of greed and self-indulgence. Blind Pharisee! First clean the inside of the cup, so that the outside of it may also become clean.

Woe to you, scribes and Pharisees, hypocrites! You are like whitewashed tombs, which appear beautiful on the outside, but inside are full of the bones of the dead and every kind of impurity. In the same way, on the outside you seem righteous to people, but inside you are full of hypocrisy and lawlessness.

Matthew 23:25–28

I have written stories on the internet for more than thirteen years. That basically makes me a blogging dinosaur. Back in the day there were conferences and gatherings and meetups for every kind of online writing. Cooking and food, parenting, tech reviews, outdoors—you name it. As my writing didn't fit within one particular niche, I felt welcome to attend any and all of these gatherings. I always had so much fun interacting with other bloggers who understood the call of a blinking cursor, the struggle with particular social algorithms, and how exciting it was to partner with new brands. I left each gathering filled up and inspired to tap on the keys again.

be a person of integrity

However, it didn't take long to see that for some people, online writing was a cover-up for who they really were.

At nearly every gathering of bloggers, one could count on a few things: seeing phones out and in use, having coffee served, and encountering a standoffish person who did not match their online persona. I will never forget a few of the awkward encounters I had with people I believed to be friendly and kind based on their online writing, only to find that they were cold and condescending.

I never expected it, and being snubbed felt like a slap in the face every time.

These encounters forced me to look honestly at my online writing and interactions and to make a choice. I could be an ideal version of myself on the internet—bubbly and charming, kind and welcoming—then remove that mask in real life and don another. Or I could share my whole self online and maintain my integrity.

The privilege of our influence is a calling and a gift, therefore we need to give our authentic, true selves—both online and off. Otherwise any influence we have is a sham. It's not only about the words we say, type, or share; it's about the actual offline or behind-the-screen lives we lead. In every part of our lives, our influence and integrity must go hand in hand.

—ANNA RENDELL

Have you encountered someone who was completely different in real life from the persona they portrayed on social media or to the public? How did it make you feel to experience that disconnect?

78

It's interesting that at the beginning of Matthew 23, Jesus acknowledges that "the teachers of religious law and the Pharisees are the official interpreters of the law of Moses," and as such, they are the people who ought to practice and obey what they are told. However, Jesus goes on to say, "Don't follow their example. For they don't practice what they teach" (vv. 2–3 NLT).

They don't practice what they teach. Let those words sink in for a minute.

These are the faith leaders at that time—the ones who teach in the synagogues (i.e., churches), who interpret the Scriptures and preach about them to the people. They hold power and influence in their communities because of their status and credentials.

But their lives don't reflect the faith they profess.

For most of Matthew 23, Jesus calls out the hypocrisy of the Pharisees and other religious teachers. They are more concerned with how they look and how others ought to behave, missing the point of what the Mosaic law was for and how to live it out faithfully.

In verses 13–15, Jesus accuses them of being religious gatekeepers, not allowing others to enter the kingdom of God and refusing to go in themselves.

In verses 23–24, Jesus exposes the nearsightedness of being exact in calculating their tithe while missing the bigger picture of what's important—justice, mercy, and faith.

In verses 25–28, Jesus points out the inconsistency of their gleaming outward appearance to what's going on inside—greed, self-indulgence, hypocrisy, and lawlessness.

These sobering words aren't just for "them"—that is, pointing fingers at someone else—but for us as well. How many times have we judged someone else's sin as worse than ours? When have we been exact about our ten-percent tithe but have sidelined issues of justice? How often have we portrayed ourselves as happy, wise, and put-together to create content for social media, when in reality we're struggling with depression and lack direction in our own lives? We're not immune to the hypocrisy of the Pharisees, but that's when we look to Jesus for mercy and help.

As you read about the Pharisees, what inconsistencies might God be asking you to address in your own life?

Write a prayer of confession, acknowledging how your lack of integrity might have hurt others and asking God to realign the way you live with your values and faith.

The Pharisees were supposed to lead the people in God's ways, but they often misused the influence they had. Jesus responds in anger and anguish, but He does so not to condemn them but to save them and those they lead. He warns them as He had warned His own disciples in Matthew 18:6, "But if you cause one of these little ones who trusts in me to fall into sin, it would be better for you to have a large millstone tied around your neck and be drowned in the depths of the sea" (NLT).

Jesus grieves over the religious leaders' hypocrisy because they believe they are well and holy but are indeed sick. They need Jesus, but they can't see it. Their misguided influence has an effect on the whole city, and Jesus weeps over Jerusalem and its people (Luke 19:41).

When we have blind spots, it's hard to see where we've gone wrong, and so in His mercy and grace toward us, God points them out so we can change. Change can only come after first becoming aware of our wrong, then acknowledging it and turning away from it.

Anna realized the weight of responsibility in handling her influence, and she had to take a good look at herself to check if she was lacking integrity. We all need to be sober-minded and aware of our blind spots, and when we still can't see correctly, may we be soft to receiving rebuke, even when it hurts to hear it.

Jesus's response of anger and anguish is the correct way to lament misuse of influence or power. What do you see in the church, your community, or yourself that should be responded to with anger and anguish?

Because we are all interconnected by our proximity to and relationships with others, the way we handle our influence affects every person we're linked to. The problem with curating a life that seems uncomplicated or only superficially vulnerable is that eventually the burden to keep it up will consume or crush us.

Our inner life and our outward actions of faith must mirror each other in order for our influence to have the impact we want for the kingdom of God. And influence carries with it a responsibility we all must be accountable for.

> **Our inner life and our outward actions of faith must mirror each other in order for our influence to have the impact we want for the kingdom of God.**

We won't do it perfectly, but we can do it with humility and awareness.

Read Proverbs 16:18. How might pride get in the way of us living with integrity?

When God shows you an area in your life where you lack integrity, how can you courageously process the rebuke so you can use your influence well?

Reflect on this prayer and make it your own today:

Lord, I admit how often I look and live more like the religious leaders of Jesus's day than I do like Jesus. I acknowledge how I have acted "Christian" for the approval of others and to prove my devotion to You. Instead of relying on appearances, help me to live a life of integrity—of living the kind of faith I profess to have. I want my influence to stem from an inner life that truly reflects the love of Jesus. Amen.

Then Saul had his own military clothes put on David. He put a bronze helmet on David's head and had him put on armor. David strapped his sword on over the military clothes and tried to walk, but he was not used to them. "I can't walk in these," David said to Saul, "I'm not used to them." So David took them off. Instead, he took his staff in his hand and chose five smooth stones from the wadi and put them in the pouch, in his shepherd's bag. Then, with his sling in his hand, he approached the Philistine.

1 Samuel 17:38–40

B efore stepping up onto the stage to talk to a room full of moms, I told myself, "Don't blink." I'd been through communication classes more than once, and my excessive blinking came up every single time.

Call it a tic or a nervous habit that I picked up somewhere along the way, but whatever it was, I could not seem to stop doing it. I was told it was distracting, and pretty soon it distracted me to the point of disqualifying myself. I told myself good communicators don't blink like there's a bug in their eyes every time they speak.

Sometimes the smallest things reveal our biggest barriers.

My insecurity wasn't really about the blinking. It was about who I believed I needed to be, look like, and sound like. I believed I wasn't cut out for speaking because I wasn't like everyone else I knew who did it. I moved from blinking too much to disliking my voice and the way I used my hands, and eventually to disliking myself.

While it's good to learn from others, it's important that we not assimilate every aspect of ourselves to be like them.

I thought about the way Jesus's very being and presence arrived in an unusual and unexpected way throughout His ministry. Instead of being described as handsome or popular, He was called lowly and unmemorable in His appearance. Though He had access to all the power in the universe, He was known to be gentle, and He often went away to rest and pray. There's no mention of charisma or charm or whether He used His hands well when He spoke. Maybe that's because such things shouldn't matter to us as much as we let them.

I mentioned my blinking to a friend who was in a communication class with me. She said she noticed it, but it didn't bother her. "It's just one of those things that makes you you. It's what you do when you speak."

The next time I was asked to speak, I said yes. Months later, after practicing my notes and working on my eye expression, I noticed my blinking while onstage. I paused, then kept speaking, remembering that what makes me me is exactly what God wants to use.

—TASHA JUN

In what ways have you disqualified yourself because you thought you needed to be like someone else to have influence?

In 1 Samuel 17, we meet David, the youngest of Jesse's eight sons, the one overlooked by his father and brothers but chosen by God to be the next king of Israel.

The Philistines—the enemy of the Israelites at that time—had a giant of a man named Goliath on their side, and twice each day for forty days Goliath would march out in front of the Israelite army, strutting about to intimidate them.

While on an errand for his father, David witnesses Goliath challenging the Israelites to send someone over to fight him and settle the battle in single combat.

David, hearing about the reward King Saul had ready for the man who could kill Goliath, takes up the challenge and tells the king, "Don't let anyone be discouraged by him; your servant will go and fight this Philistine!" (17:32).

King Saul refuses, but David persists and convinces him to let him fight Goliath. Saul tries to outfit David with his own armor and sword, but they don't fit. Instead, David takes the armor he knows: five smooth stones, his shepherd's staff, a sling, and the assurance that God is with him.

Out of fear or intimidation, we might try to put on another person's way of talking or behaving or leading in order to legitimize our influence. Or perhaps, like Tasha, we might try to strip away parts of who we are in order to prove that our influence is the kind that people need or want.

David knew that he needed only to be himself and that he could defeat Goliath because he fought in the Lord's name (17:45). In the same way, our confidence to influence others comes from an inner strength of knowing who we are and how God made us.

What kind of "armor" do you hide behind to feel more legitimate in your influence? Some examples could be education/degrees, job titles,

accomplishments, experiences, or relationship statuses. How would it feel not to put on that armor?

_____

_____

_____

_____

Tasha's blinking revealed an underlying barrier for her: she felt unqualified to influence others through her speaking. Her barriers were internal, whereas David's were external and came from those who were closest to him.

The first barrier was Eliab, his oldest brother. When he sees David coming to bring the brothers some food, Eliab demands, "Why did you come down here? Who did you leave those few sheep with in the wilderness? I know your arrogance and your evil heart—you came down to see the battle!" (17:28).

He spits these accusations at David, perhaps out of jealousy for not being chosen by the Lord as Israel's next king despite being Jesse's firstborn son (1 Sam. 16:6). Or perhaps he can't stand how King Saul favors David, the baby of the family (16:14–22).

But David isn't intimidated by Eliab or by Goliath. He doesn't cower from his oldest brother's sharp words or the taunts of the Philistine giant. He stands his ground, undergirded by recalling the times God had been with him in the past.

When he was faithfully shepherding his father's sheep, David had fought off danger and death. He had protected the sheep from lions and bears. And though David may have been the youngest, it was precisely during the unseen times that God had been preparing, strengthening, and sharpening his skills. He isn't afraid of Goliath or put down by Eliab because God has prepared him for this moment.

David armed himself with his slingshot and the assurance that God was with him. What unique tools (skills, experiences, or talents) has the Lord given you to influence others just as you are?

Read 1 Samuel 17:34–37. How does being faithful to the tasks at hand lead to authority in our influence?

David responds to his brother Eliab and to King Saul with confidence and authority. He protests Eliab's accusations by asking, "What have I done now?" (17:29). He knows to let Eliab's words slide off his back. When brought before King Saul, he persists in his determination to fight Goliath, listing the ways God raised him up to be a fighter against the impossible while he had been shepherding his father's sheep.

Saul looks at David as just a boy, but David knows that his years of faithfulness in the mundane have laid the foundation for his trust in God. His faithfulness and dependence on God give him authority and impact—particularly on King Saul, and later as a leader for the Israelites.

David may have looked like he was going up against Goliath bare and vulnerable without Saul's heavy armor. Perhaps he even looked foolish with his slingshot and stones. But David went out armed with God's power. His confidence was in the One who had given him victory before, and he knew God would come through again.

We can courageously face our giants, whatever they might be, knowing that God has been preparing us for these moments all our lives.

We don't need to be like anyone else in how we influence others. We can courageously face our giants, whatever they might be, knowing that God has been preparing us for these moments all our lives. We don't go out alone. Our God is with us, and we can trust Him to go before us as well.

Read David's reply to Goliath's challenge in 1 Samuel 17:45–47. Write your own battle cry to the Goliaths in your life.

It can feel vulnerable to be who we are without hiding behind someone else's armor. What does it look like for you to be a woman of influence who courageously shows up fully as yourself?

Reflect on this prayer and make it your own today:

Lord, thank You that I don't have to be like anyone else in order to have influence. Thank You for the ways You've made me unique in my skills, my gifts, my upbringing, and even my quirks. Help me to be faithful in where You've called me to be right now, so that when I am called into bigger battles, I can confidently go in Your name. Amen.

After this, Jesus traveled around Galilee. He wanted to stay out of Judea, where the Jewish leaders were plotting his death. But soon it was time for the Jewish Festival of Shelters, and Jesus' brothers said to him, "Leave here and go to Judea, where your followers can see your miracles! You can't become famous if you hide like this! If you can do such wonderful things, show yourself to the world!" For even his brothers didn't believe in him.

John 7:1–5 NLT

I'm a connector. It brings me so much joy to connect with people, to connect people with other people, and to connect people with their callings. But it took me a little while to arrive at this place.

In my years of following Christ and being part of the church, I have been misunderstood a good bit. We all have at times. But there is something about being misunderstood regarding the way God has wired me that is especially hurtful.

I have had well-meaning friends make passing comments about my wanting influence with certain people or intentionally trying to situate myself into places with people of influence.

Every one of those comments wounded me, and I realized that sometimes it's the people we're closest to who shout the loudest accusations and doubts about our identities and motives. As I sifted through those comments, I realized how much I was wanting the approval of others instead of leaning into my identity in Christ, regardless of who understood it.

Out of the pain of being misunderstood, I learned that in those kinds of situations, I have to make a choice: I can either shrink back in fear, shame, and insecurity, or I can stand tall in confidence, trust, and security.

God made me a connector of people, and the connections I've made haven't been random. Each one was ordained by Him, and I have been blessed by them and have been a blessing to them. When people close to me question my motives, I know I'm not the only one in that boat.

Jesus had so many people in His life who didn't understand Him, approve of Him, or even believe Him. His own hometown topped the list of doubters. They assumed things and judged Him based on their past knowledge and experience of Him, and they couldn't see Him for who He was because of their limited perspective.

But Jesus knew His purpose and His identity as the Son of God, and He kept going in ministry, secure in that identity.

People may doubt who I was made to be, but I know that God put me on this earth to bring people together, to be the one to reach out to people who are unseen, and to help them know their God-given identity and live it confidently. My joy is found not in proving myself to the doubters but in faithfully doing the will of God in my life.

—KARINA ALLEN

Have you experienced someone close to you doubting your gifts or purpose in life? How did that make you feel?

After feeding more than five thousand people, Jesus then teaches in the synagogue, and the crowds who witnessed that miracle, along with those who follow Jesus, listen to Him teach about being the "bread of life" that came down from heaven (John 6:35–40).

But as His message becomes harder to understand and accept, the people start to doubt Him, saying, "Isn't this Jesus, the son of Joseph? We know his father and mother. How can he say, 'I came down from heaven'?" (6:42 NLT).

Even those who follow Jesus question His message, and they begin to complain about how hard it is to understand. Jesus, knowing their disbelief, tells them plainly that not everyone will believe Him (6:64). Offended, many of them leave, and Jesus turns to His closest disciples—the twelve He had hand-picked—and asks, "Are you also going to leave?" (6:67).

But the clincher comes in the Scripture passage for today.

Jesus wants to avoid going to Judea because the Jewish leaders are plotting His death. But His brothers, completely unaware of the situation and not understanding who Jesus really is, mock Him about hiding. They tell Him, "Leave here and go to Judea, where your followers can see your miracles! You can't become famous if you hide like this! If you can do such wonderful things, show yourself to the world!" (John 7:3–4 NLT).

Essentially, they're telling Jesus that He's not doing the fame thing right. Like the crowds who were filled by the fish and loaves, perhaps they believe Jesus's purpose is to be the next ruling king (6:15). And if so, He should obviously be showing up and working the crowds instead of hiding. Can't you just imagine them rolling their eyes at their older brother, telling Him to prove Himself if He's so great?

Sometimes the ones closest to us—those who have seen us grow up, who have access to our daily lives or know our backstories—doubt us the most. But their reactions don't determine our identity or our purpose. Neither are we to bend this way and that to others' thoughts about us, particularly when their words seem to go against God's word to us.

Read the following verses. What do these passages tell you about your identity and God's purposes for your life?

> John 15:15
>
> Ephesians 2:10
>
> Philippians 4:13

How can you apply the truths you read in those passages to the hurtful things that others have said about you?

Jesus doesn't argue with His brothers about who He is. He doesn't sit them down as the eldest in the family (and as God Himself) to lecture them about His virtues and His place in the world. Instead, He simply says, "Now is not the right time for me to go, but you can go anytime. The world can't hate you, but it does hate me because I accuse it of doing evil. You go on. I'm not going to this festival, because my time has not yet come" (John 7:6–8 NLT).

Jesus, in all divine wisdom, simply tells His brothers it's not time. In that statement, He rejects their advice to Him and distinguishes the difference between Himself and them. They function by what they can see (the crowds following Jesus), while Jesus functions by the unseen (the will of the Father). It isn't His time to go, so He doesn't go when His brothers tell Him to.

Eventually, Jesus goes to the festival, but He does so secretly instead of publicly (7:10).

When we are aware of God's leading and are in tune with the Spirit, we can stand our ground even when others are telling us what may seem to be the logical or even wise thing to do. Like Karina's confidence in her calling to connect people, we can be sure of God's plan for who we interact with and influence—and when we do so—despite what others might think. And in His timing, we will never be too early or too late to fulfill His purpose for our lives.

> **In God's timing, we will never be too early or too late to fulfill His purpose for our lives.**

Read John 14:10. Jesus did as God the Father told Him to do. What can we learn from Jesus's example of listening and obeying God instead of being swayed by people's doubts about Him?

Despite some of His followers leaving Him, despite the doubts of His brothers, Jesus continues the work the Father sent Him to do. He teaches, He heals, He restores lives. Unfortunately, the people continue to be divided over Him. Some believe Him, and others want to kill Him.

The way God gives you influence may not look like Karina's gift for connecting people or Jesus's abilities to teach and heal. Instead, God may call you to make a difference in the lives of your coworkers, children, friends, or church—and others might not understand why you choose to invest in those people or places over the ones they think you should pick.

Unfortunately, those who cannot see what God is doing in us will often try to pull us down or convince us of their logic and concern for us. Even Jesus's own family said He was crazy in an attempt to excuse His behavior (Mark 3:21). But at the end of the day, we must choose to invest in the people God leads us to with the gifts and skills He's given us, despite what others may say about us.

We are women of influence—called and able to use our God-given abilities to make Him known. When people discredit us and doubt the change we can bring about, let's remember who God made us to be and trust that He will use our influence as He sees fit.

It takes courage to go against what people say about you—even when they're wrong. What would it look like for you to continue influencing others just as God created you to do, despite what others say?

_____

_____

_____

_____

Reflect on this prayer and make it your own today:

Lord, thank You for making me who I am. Thank You that Your word over me is the final word. Help me when people's doubts speak louder than Your voice, and give me courage to be confident in how You made me to influence others. Amen.

For God has not given us a spirit of fear, but one of power, love, and sound judgment.

2 Timothy 1:7

We were gathered on Monica's porch on a crisp spring morning—a close circle of friends I affectionately call a pile of iron. Sandra, a longtime friend of Monica's we'd only "met" by reputation, was there as well. She was a woman of wisdom, wholly devoted to Jesus. As coffee's magical aroma filled the air, we settled around the table with breakfast plates full.

None of us were interested in skimming the surface of conversation, so we went deep fast. As each friend opened her heart, the others listened and poured in grace, encouragement, and truth.

I was eager to share because I was wrestling old demons, the ones that tell credible lies I'm quick to believe:

Because I haven't had equal accomplishment to my peers, I am a failure.

What I have to offer doesn't matter.

I'm not actually qualified to do what I'm doing.

Maybe I don't have what it takes to be successful, and my efforts are wasted time.

Was it time for me to return to a traditional job? After all, it had been years since I had a regular writing routine, and my readers were dwindling in direct proportion to my publishing consistency. Though I hadn't actually pursued a writing *career*, for some inexplicable reason I allowed arbitrary social media numbers to define me. I was buying into a mythical comparison that didn't even make sense.

I may have known better in my head, but it took a new friend to press it into my heart.

"How many people follow you?" Sandra queried. I answered her, and she continued, "Don't you think Satan would love to defeat you, to stifle encouraging even a fraction of your readers who might turn to Jesus in response?"

Her question lingered in the air as I contemplated her wisdom. Satan would love for us to measure our influence as all or nothing, to believe that if we can't impact everyone, we impact no one. But Scripture says that God calls us by name, and when we respond to Him, we're indwelled by His Spirit. We're forever changed.

God gives us a spirit of power, not timidity. He's given each of us a unique voice and story to point others to Him and to use our influence to impact our world for His glory.

What a great reminder that the number of friends and followers is never the point. Whether I have ten or ten thousand, I am to point others to Jesus by the authority He's given me, and that is always the point.

—ROBIN DANCE

Read 2 Timothy 1:7. What does having a spirit of power and not fear mean to you?

_____

_____

_____

_____

Paul writes this second letter to Timothy, whom he had raised as his spiritual son. As Paul faces imminent death (4:6), he writes to encourage, prepare, and commission Timothy for the work ahead as a young leader in the church.

In the first chapter of the letter, where we find our passage for today, Paul reminds Timothy of who he is—his faith, his heritage, and his calling. In order to understand the depth and weight of verse 7, of not having a spirit of fear and timidity, we need to read what comes before.

In verse 5, Paul commends Timothy for his trust in the Lord—a faith that was passed down from his mother, Eunice, and his grandmother, Lois. He was shaped by their influence and the environment they had created in the home, and now he carries within himself a generational legacy of faith.

And because of this, Paul encourages Timothy to "rekindle the gift of God that is in you through the laying on of my hands" (v. 6). He affirms the work God has already started in Timothy and tells him to keep at it.

Thus, the foundation to have a spirit of power, love, and sound judgment comes from what God has *already* established within Timothy.

The same goes for us. We don't need to grasp at external factors to give us power in our influence with others, love to impact others with care, or sound judgment to be sober-minded in how we use our platforms. We have the Holy Spirit within us to help us fight fear and timidity.

We saw how Robin looked to her social media numbers as a measure of the influence she had. What external factors have you depended on to measure your influence with others?

Since the power of our influence comes from within, as evidenced in 2 Timothy 1:7, how does that change the focus and/or motivation of your efforts in building influence with others?

_____

_____

_____

_____

It's to be expected that we will struggle with integrity when the message we hear from others is to focus on our outward appearance and the number of followers we have—both online and in person. Often, those two factors are the standards for measuring the success of our influence, even within the church, and the results are telling.

Whenever the focus of our efforts is geared toward accessorizing what's on the outside, we lose our way. We get caught up in the latest advice on how to build our influence instead of keeping our focus on the work God has started within us.

> **Rekindling a fire requires constant tending, and so do the gifts God gives us.**

The work of rekindling a fire requires constant tending. If you become distracted by other tasks or goals and neglect the fire, the flames will quickly burn out. But if you focus on the fire, stoking and stirring it constantly, it will burn brightly. So it is with the gifts God gives us.

For example, if God has given you the gift of teaching, it doesn't do any good for you or your listeners if you only look the part of a teacher. You might have a hefty study Bible, respond to difficult questions with the right answers, post Scripture verses for others to see, or even guide others in their walk with Jesus. But if you don't study the Bible and learn how to teach it well, if the Word of God doesn't transform you and shape the way you live your life, having the gift is meaningless.

We become people of integrity and influence when we resist the temptation to focus on outward appearances and instead keep at the work God has started within us. Often, the work is done internally and is unseen, but integrity doesn't start on the outside and work its way inward. It starts from within and makes what we do on the outside mean something more than just appearances.

Read Proverbs 11:3. How should integrity guide the way we influence people?

In Robin's story, the lies she lists come from underlying fears of unimportance and insignificance. Sandra lovingly tells her the truth that her influence isn't about numbers but about everyone who might turn to Jesus in response to something Robin has shared.

When we get wrapped up in what influence "should" look like, we lose peace of mind. The New King James Version of 2 Timothy 1:7 reads, "For God has not given us a spirit of fear, but of power and of love and of a *sound mind*."

A sound mind comes from living a life of integrity—when who we proclaim to be matches who we actually are. When there's a lack of integrity, truth becomes blurred. Right motivations are difficult to distinguish. Correction becomes offensive and difficult to accept, and influence becomes more about us and less about God.

When we can recognize that influence comes from the Spirit of God within us, from having a spirit of power, love, and a sound mind, fears and lies lose their strength. Our focus corrects itself, and we see that having influence isn't for our benefit but for God's glory.

Write out 2 Timothy 1:7 from the New King James Version. What does having a sound mind look like to you?

What are some red flags you can look out for that indicate you've started to rely on external measures to prove your influence instead of trusting in the Spirit of God within you?

Reflect on this prayer and make it your own today:

God, sometimes fear drives me to perform or to live a life that doesn't demonstrate integrity. I know it's not how I should live, but it's easy to get caught up in the game of becoming influential. When I lose my way, remind me that my power comes from within, from the work You have already started in me. Help me to influence others from that place of peace. Amen.

"Therefore, go. I am sending you to Pharaoh so that you may lead my people, the Israelites, out of Egypt."

But Moses asked God, "Who am I that I should go to Pharaoh and that I should bring the Israelites out of Egypt?"

He answered, "I will certainly be with you, and this will be the sign to you that I am the one who sent you: when you bring the people out of Egypt, you will all worship God at this mountain."

Exodus 3:10–12

It was my first Sunday on the job, and I was being introduced to the congregation as "Pastor Grace." But the title felt false. I hadn't gotten a master of divinity degree from my seminary, nor was I ordained. It was meant to be a title of respect and authority for those under my care in ministry, but instead it made me feel like an impostor.

I had arrived at my Korean immigrant church with a master's degree in world missions, planning to develop a program that would help reach unreached people groups around the globe. As a child of missionary parents, I had dreamed of this kind of work, the impact it would have for God's kingdom, and how I would fulfill my life's purpose of doing overseas missions work.

But it never came to be. The present needs of the church didn't require a missions director but a pastor—one who could disciple others, hold space for those who had been hurt by the church, and even preach. They needed someone who could minister to children *and* adults, who could see those on the margins and pursue them.

My eyes had long been trained to look for the ones who came in alone and nervously chose a seat in the back, who didn't look comfortable making small talk after the service, and who were quick to escape as soon as they could.

I grew up as a pastor's kid and a missionary kid, serving alongside my parents, leading when there was no one else to lead, teaching and caring for others since I was ten. And as the second of four kids, I was often the go-between child in the family. I could readily understand and empathize with both sides when there was an argument. Family and friends felt comfortable to share their burdens, knowing I could and would hold space for their frustrations, anger, and grief.

Someone once told me I was an old soul stuck in a child's body, and I had wondered what good that was when I was younger. But as I found my groove as "Pastor Grace," I realized that's who I had been for so much of my life. The ability to see others and their needs, to welcome them with open arms, and the desire to lead and teach all started when I was barely in fourth grade.

Even though I'm not a pastor anymore, it's still the role I play for those around me—when I write, when I meet my mentees for coffee, when I lead a Bible study, when I feed my family and teach my kids how to love each other better. I'm not pretending to be someone I'm not; I'm exactly who I was meant to be.

—GRACE P. CHO

Think about the last time you felt like an impostor. What were the surrounding circumstances, and why did you feel that way?

When we meet Moses in Exodus 3, he has a complicated history. He was an Israelite, born into slavery in Egypt. In an effort to spare his life, his mother placed him in a basket in the Nile River, where he was discovered by the daughter of Pharaoh. Though Pharaoh had given the order to kill all Israelite baby boys, she was moved by his cries and adopted him as her own. So Moses grew up with prestige and privilege—a life completely opposite from that of his people.

One day, in an ill-conceived effort to stand up for his own, Moses killed an Egyptian whom he witnessed beating a Hebrew slave. He thought what he'd done was a secret, but word got out and he had to flee from Egypt, losing everything—his identity, his family, his life as he knew it.

Moses settled in the desert land of Midian, where he got married and settled down. It's in this mundane season of life, while tending his father-in-law's sheep, that God met Moses in a burning bush.

Knowing his history, we can understand why Moses responded to God as he did: "Who am I that I should go to Pharaoh and that I should bring the Israelites out of Egypt?" (Exod. 3:11). He couldn't see how or why he would be qualified to lead the Israelites to freedom.

How many times have we asked ourselves the same question when we've felt called to something big or impossible?

Who am I to sing in front of a crowd?

Who am I to raise my children when I have no idea what I'm doing?

Who am I to speak out about a leader who's done wrong to me?

Who am I to share my story when so many other people have more powerful testimonies to share?

The list could go on and on.

A thousand reasons might prove why you're not qualified, but when God asks you to do something, all He's looking for is a yes.

How does feeling like an impostor come down to what you fear?

Our fears don't keep God from asking us to use our influence to lead others. What promise did God give Moses in Exodus 3:12 that encourages you to face your fears?

Feeling like an impostor doesn't mean we *are* impostors. An impostor is someone who pretends to be someone they are not. For Grace, being called a pastor made her feel like an impostor, but she wasn't. Not only did she have the gifts and skills to be a pastor, but she even had the position and the title given to her.

> **A thousand reasons might prove why you're not qualified, but when God asks you to do something, all He's looking for is a yes.**

In Exodus 3:12, God answers Moses's question of "Who am I?" with words of assurance: "I will certainly be with you, and this will be the sign to you that I am the one who sent you: when you bring the people out of Egypt, you will all worship God at this mountain."

God gives a promise and a guarantee. Moses might've been seeking an answer to *why* God had chosen him, but God answers with the only qualification that he needs—God's with-ness. He can see behind the question to the underlying fear in Moses's heart, and He directs His answer toward it. *Don't worry. I will be with you, Moses. And to prove that I am, you will come back here to this very mountain where I've called you with the people you will set free.*

God doesn't lay impossible tasks on us and then watch from a distance to see how we do. He is with us—in the darkest and lowest moments, in the overwhelming loneliness, in the lack and inadequacy we feel. And His with-ness is more than just waving pom-poms and cheering us on from the sidelines. His with-ness equips us and helps us along the way.

Write down some of your own "Who am I?" questions. Then, next to each one, write God's answer: *I will certainly be with you.* **How does that affect your confidence in the role God has given you?**

_____

_____

_____

_____

When God calls us to be or do something, denying what He says about us exposes our lack of faith and a double-mindedness. In other words, if we say we trust God but then balk when we actually have to trust Him, we cannot say we're the same inside and out. Our integrity becomes compromised.

In Grace's story, she had what it took to be a pastor on the inside and the correct title to match it on the outside. The only problem was that she couldn't wrap her mind around it and just believe. Perhaps you've experienced similar doubts about yourself when you've had the experience and promotion to be a manager at your job but you still felt unqualified. Or perhaps you felt you weren't fit to be a small group facilitator at church even though your leaders chose you because of your faithfulness and maturity.

Too often, we're foolish enough to think that we know more than God. We might shy away from opportunities to influence others and think we're being humble. But instead our pride and lack of trust in God prevent us from having the impact we want to have through our faith.

The words of Jesus ring especially true when this happens: "Why are you afraid, you of little faith?" (Matt. 8:26). When opportunities come for us to rise up in faith, may we not resist God's invitation. Instead, let's believe His words over us, trusting that He is who He is—and He knows what He's doing when He calls you to lead. As God told Moses, "I AM WHO I AM. . . . This is my name forever; this is how I am to be remembered in every generation" (Exod. 3:14–15). He has not changed since then.

God won't always show up in burning bushes, but when He speaks, may we reply in faith, "Here I am!"

How has God's faithful presence given you courage to face a difficult task?

Reflect on this prayer and make it your own today:

Lord, thank You for the times when You invite me to something that feels impossible. You stretch my faith, making it more resilient, and You always prove Yourself to me. Thank You for trusting me to impact others for Your kingdom and for equipping me along the way. Help me to believe when it's hard to see why You would choose me, and may my heart be willing to say yes in faith. Amen.

be generous with your influence

Later that same day Jesus left the house and sat beside the lake. A large crowd soon gathered around him, so he got into a boat. Then he sat there and taught as the people stood on the shore. He told many stories in the form of parables, such as this one:

"Listen! A farmer went out to plant some seeds. As he scattered them across his field, some seeds fell on a footpath, and the birds came and ate them. Other seeds fell on shallow soil with underlying rock. The seeds sprouted quickly because the soil was shallow. But the plants soon wilted under the hot sun, and since they didn't have deep roots, they died. Other seeds fell among thorns that grew up and choked out the tender plants. Still other seeds fell on fertile soil, and they produced a crop that was thirty, sixty, and even a hundred times as much as had been planted! Anyone with ears to hear should listen and understand."

Matthew 13:1–9 NLT

I live in Silicon Valley among a diverse community who work in high tech. My kids go to public school, and it is an intentional choice. My husband and I believe our children's school community is our mission field. Every day, school pickup is a golden opportunity to chat with women who wouldn't step foot in a church.

Most often I spend that time chatting with other moms about ordinary topics like homework, favorite places to eat out, and plans for the weekend, which seems far from anything spiritual. But cultivating relationships *is* spiritual work as we learn to love our neighbors.

One day, God put a particular mom on my heart. She and her family had moved to California from China, and she had a boy around my son Caleb's age. Perhaps it was our shared ethnic identity or simply that my heart goes out to those who are quiet and unseen, but I wanted to make sure she and her family felt welcome in our community.

For the first year, we exchanged no more than a few words here and there. I wanted to get to know her better, but she seemed very shy and uninterested in chatting. I hoped over time that saying hi and giving her a warm smile would lead to cultivating a deeper friendship, but it didn't happen right away.

Thankfully, our boys were able to become friends, and we had the opportunity to invite their family over for their first American Thanksgiving dinner. With each connection we made, our family prayed for a chance to share the gospel with them.

It wasn't until two years later that we had the chance to do so.

I was standing outside the classroom when this mom came up to chat with me. She had noticed that our family was particularly kind and cheerful, and she asked what I had done to nurture this kindness in my boys.

It was the opening to a conversation I had prayed for. After years of planting seeds of hope through our conversations, never really knowing if they were going anywhere, I was able to share with her that we were a family who values being loving and kind because we follow Jesus, who is loving and kind. I asked her if she might be curious about what Christians believe and said I'd love to introduce her to it all. She surprised me with a yes and asked if her husband could join as well.

Imagine our joy when my husband and I sat down to share the gospel with this couple while Caleb got to share about his faith to their son in the next room!

We are meant to be generous with ourselves because that is what Jesus did. And who knows whom we will impact as a result?

—BONNIE GRAY

Have you ever been surprised by how someone was affected by your influence in their life? If so, what are some ways you had that unexpected impact?

Nancy: I meeting for the first time.

In Matthew 13, Jesus tells the parable of the sower to teach about how the Word of God lands on the ears of those who hear it. Some are like the path, hardened and unable to receive the Word or understand it. Some are like shallow soil, where the message is received but is not rooted deeply. Some are like the thorny ground, where the Word is choked out by worries and temptations around them. And yet, some are like the fertile soil, where the message is received, takes deep root, and produces a plentiful harvest (vv. 19–23).

The part of the parable we want to focus on today is *how* the farmer sows the seeds. In the New Living Translation, verse 4 says that he scattered them across his field. The Greek word translated as "scattered" is *skorpizo*, and it means to "fly in every direction."[1] The farmer holds a handful of seeds and lets them fall where they may. There are various ways to plant seeds, but this way lends itself to spreading the seeds generously and trusting that there will be fruit when they land in the right place.

We can liken the seeds to our influence with those around us—particularly our influence as carriers of the gospel.

If we believe in the good news of Jesus, our own hearts have been fertile soil that received the gospel message and were truly transformed. As a result, we are meant to multiply exponentially—"thirty, sixty, and even a hundred times as much as had been planted!" (13:23). One seed can grow a plant that produces many flowers—each flower holding the potential to bear fruit, and within each fruit, a handful of seeds. Thus from the one seed can come an abundant harvest. Imagine the impact we can have when we generously scatter the seeds of our influence!

Think about the people in your own sphere and the various spheres you travel in—perhaps your children's school, like Bonnie, or your workplace, or your own family. How might you sow seeds of the gospel in those places?

Read Matthew 28:18–20. Why is it imperative that we scatter our influence generously?

Having an impact on someone's life isn't a guarantee. As the parable of the sower tells us, people's hearts may not be in the best condition to receive truth, and as with plants, timing is crucial. In Bonnie's story, she didn't force the mom to hear her out or manipulate a welcome so she could preach at her. Even though God had put this woman on her heart, Bonnie was patient and waited for the right moment to invite her to learn more.

We never know when a word spoken or a kindness shared may have lasting impact on someone or even lay the groundwork for us to share about Jesus with them. We may not see results for years. We may not ever get to see results at all. But as we're urged in Galatians 6:9, "Let us not get tired of doing good, for we will reap at the proper time if we don't give up."

There will be times when we scatter our seeds of influence and they land in fertile soil we didn't expect. Matthew 8:5–13 tells us about a Roman officer who came to Jesus and pleaded for Him to heal his servant. The Romans ruled Israel at the time and thus were considered enemies of the Jews. However, in desperation, the Roman officer turned to Jesus, knowing what He could do. In verse 8, he says, "Lord, I am not worthy to have you come into my home. Just say the word from where you are, and my servant will be healed" (NLT).

> **We never know when a word spoken or a kindness shared may have lasting impact on someone.**

The Roman officer clearly understood Jesus's power to heal and His position of authority. He submitted himself to Jesus and asked for help, and Jesus responded by saying He had not seen faith like this in all of Israel (8:10).

Jesus's own people had hearts like the hard path, unwilling to believe Him, but this Roman officer had a heart that was soft and ready to receive, and because of it, his servant was healed by Jesus's power.

Our hearts can be any of the types of soil we read about in Matthew 13:1–9. Which soil do you currently identify your heart with and why?

Jesus ends the parable of the sower by saying, "Let anyone who has ears listen" (Matt. 13:9). When our ears are tuned to how culture defines influence and teaches us to influence others (even if it's for a good cause), it's often about how we can control or manipulate a situation for our benefit. It's easy to become tightfisted or to be hesitant to do something because we're afraid we'll do it wrong.

We can learn three things from Bonnie's story. First, we need to pay attention to how God is moving in our spheres of influence. Second, we need to be generous with ourselves, our time, our energy, our resources, and our relationships (e.g., family, friends, access to leaders). Third, we need to be patient for the seed to bear fruit. It might take years or decades, or you might never have the privilege of seeing the harvest. But we're not responsible for when or how the harvest comes. We are, however, called to have an open hand and to scatter our influence generously.

Of the three things we learned from Bonnie's story, which area is God showing you that you need to grow in? What might that growth look like?

Reflect on this prayer and make it your own today:

God, thank You that Jesus set the example of being generous with His influence. Give me the kind of faith that the Roman officer had, and help me to actively work against the belief that being generous is foolish and naïve. Guide me to unfurl my hands and scatter my influence with joy and freedom. Amen.

What then is Apollos? What is Paul? They are servants through whom you believed, and each has the role the LORD has given. I planted, Apollos watered, but God gave the growth. So, then, neither the one who plants nor the one who waters is anything, but only God who gives the growth. Now he who plants and he who waters are one, and each will receive his own reward according to his own labor. For we are God's coworkers. You are God's field, God's building.

1 Corinthians 3:5–9

I stood facing the wall, wiping away tears as a couple dozen moms cheerfully chatted around me. I needed to gain my composure before stepping onstage to give the official morning welcome, announcements, and prayer. *Why does this have to be so hard? Are You sure this is what You want, God?* I silently pleaded.

Carolyn, my friend and women's ministry director, spotted me.

"Another rough childcare drop-off?" she asked sympathetically.

"They had to pry Noah off my body. He was screaming when I left." Fresh tears poured down my face.

Carolyn put her arm around me and prayed encouragement over me.

I hugged my friend and grabbed the mic. It turned out to be another beautiful gathering with food, fellowship, and motherhood encouragement. Carolyn checked on Noah, and after a few minutes my spirited four-year-old was playing happily. His two little brothers were doing fine too.

Separation anxiety and tantrums weren't the only struggles that came with being the coordinator of a newly expanding moms ministry. There were challenges securing enough nursery volunteers, managing fundraising efforts, and handling weekly setup and teardown with my tornado of three littles in tow.

But I knew God was working. I heard it in the conversations around each table. I saw it in the faces of weary moms who left each meeting with hope-filled eyes. I sensed it in the friendships cultivated during playdates.

Surely these first-year growing pains would be worth it. Next year we'd expand the leadership team so the workload would be lighter. We'd recruit more mentors willing to invest in young moms. I'd find better speakers and plan new table décor.

Yes, this was just the beginning.

And it was—except I wasn't the one to see it through. At the end of the year, God abruptly called me out of my role. It was never my intention to lead the ministry for just one year, and there was no other obvious replacement. But this group wasn't mine—it was God's. He would take care of it.

And He did. Abundantly! I helped sow fresh seeds, but God called someone else to help reap the harvest. Kimberlee just finished her sixth year leading the moms group, and the things God has done during that time blow my mind! It's now the largest outreach ministry in the whole church. Kimberlee's passion and skills made all the difference.

What a joy to know that we can always trust God to bring the right workers into the field exactly when they're needed.

—BECKY KEIFE

Has this ever happened to you? Perhaps you've sown your time and energy into a group of students who graduate and move into their next season. Or maybe you've invested in an organization, but your time there was cut short by life circumstances. How did it feel to have your involvement in a ministry or project end before you expected it to?

_____

_____

_____

_____

The Corinthian church was a mess, and in chapter 3 of the first letter to the Corinthians, Paul tells them that their quarreling over which leader is better is immature and ridiculous. Imagine two groups of grown people in the church fighting over who's the better pastor—the one who planted the church (Paul) or the one who ministered after him (Apollos). Jealousy and one-upping was probably at play. Though both men clearly had significant impact in the church, Paul tells the believers that their petty fighting shows that they are acting like unbelievers (1 Cor. 3:4).

Not much has changed in today's church culture. With social media and the internet, Christian leaders have become like celebrities, with people ascribing to the teachings of so-and-so or such-and-such. People swear by them and glorify their books or their theology or their church's worship music. We are often no better than the Corinthian church back in Paul's day, arguing over who's better, who's right.

Paul corrects the Corinthians' view of himself and Apollos by saying, "[We] are servants through whom you believed, and each has the role the Lord has given" (3:5). While people wanted to elevate Paul and Apollos, Paul deflates that image by saying that they are both servants and are therefore on the same level. Each of them has a role given to

> **We're all given different roles in different seasons, but God is the one who ultimately does the growing, the leading, and the transforming.**

them by God. Neither is greater than the other, because it is God who does the growing (3:7).

As women of influence, it's easy to see how we also can get caught up in being *the* most important person—the one people look up to, praise, and want to follow. Sometimes we want to be and do all the things—mostly out of good desires—but we need to remember that we're all given different roles in different seasons. God is the one who ultimately does the growing, the leading, and the transforming.

Have you struggled with wanting to play all the roles? How does it feel to know that God is the one who does the growing and changing in people?

_____

_____

_____

_____

In this season of life, what role is God inviting you to do? Planting? Watering? Harvesting?

_____

_____

_____

_____

In 1 Corinthians 3:6, Paul writes that his job was to plant the seeds of faith. Apollos's job was to water the seeds, and it was God's job to grow the seeds. Furthermore, he says in verses 8–9 that "he who plants and he who waters are one. . . . For we are God's coworkers."

The phrase "Teamwork makes the dream work" is true. We are part of a team, with arms linked together in the work God has before us. We are not ranked into different positions, such as managers and assistant managers and employees. We are all on the same level. When we humbly recognize this, accept our roles, and do the work, we get to see the beauty of the body of Christ in motion.

Each of us has a mixture of gifts, skills, and life seasons that allows us to participate in the work God is doing. The work is His, but He desires for us to co-labor with Him and to work with one another. In doing so, we get to experience God more intimately as we work side by side with Him and more fully as we see glimpses of Him in one another.

Read 1 Corinthians 12:12–26. How have you experienced the beauty of the body of Christ in motion? (Note: it doesn't have to be in a church setting.)

In a relay race, the runners work together as a team. As one runner finishes her lap, the next is in position, ready to receive the baton and run her own lap. And when the team wins, it's not just one of them who gets to stand on the podium to receive the medal. The whole team stands together and each runner receives her own medal.

Integrated into the practice of teamwork are humility and generosity. Humility enables us to acknowledge our limits—particularly when it comes to the end of our calling. Becky hadn't planned for her time as the moms ministry coordinator to end so abruptly, nor did she have a replacement ready. But she trusted that this was God's work and that He'd take care of it. She passed the baton to Kimberlee, believing that God had equipped and chosen Kimberlee to keep the ministry going. Humility allows us to celebrate another's success, and that's what Becky was able to do.

Generosity is necessary in teamwork. When one person on a team hogs the work in order to get the glory or can't see that their time has come to an end, they are only thinking of themselves and not the team. They have made the work about themselves instead of God, and selfishness, not generosity, reigns in their heart. Genuine teamwork—not just being part of the team—means giving of ourselves freely without expecting to reap the harvest of our labor. We invest without holding back, knowing our part is important but is just one of many other parts.

Paul laid the foundation for the Corinthian church and others built upon it, but the foundation was always Christ and Christ alone. Remembering that will free us to influence others generously out of the abundant love and grace we've received in Jesus.

Read 1 Corinthians 3:5–9. As you consider the connection between generosity and influence, how does God calling you His coworker reflect His generosity?

How does courage play into influencing others, even when you might not reap the harvest?

Reflect on this prayer and make it your own today:

Lord, help me to be humble and generous when it comes to my influence and how I invest in others. Thank You for not holding back and for inviting me to be Your co-laborer. I want to be part of the work You do to make all things right in this world. Amen.

When he went ashore, he saw a large crowd and had compassion on them, because they were like sheep without a shepherd. Then he began to teach them many things.

When it grew late, his disciples approached him and said, "This place is deserted, and it is already late. Send them away so that they can go into the surrounding countryside and villages to buy themselves something to eat."

"You give them something to eat," he responded.

They said to him, "Should we go and buy two hundred denarii worth of bread and give them something to eat?"

He asked them, "How many loaves do you have? Go and see."

When they found out they said, "Five, and two fish." Then he instructed them to have all the people sit down in groups on the green grass. So they sat down in groups of hundreds and fifties. He took the five loaves and the two fish, and looking up to heaven, he blessed and broke the loaves. He kept giving them to his disciples to set before the people. He also divided the two fish among them all. Everyone ate and was satisfied.

Mark 6:34–42

One of my dear friends is an incredible author and teacher. As you can imagine, her life is busy, with a constant stream of people wanting to gain access to her. The two of us met several years ago at her church in

Nashville. We hit it off immediately and kept in touch a bit for a few months. She ended up coming close to my city to speak at a conference, so I decided to go—even though I went alone.

My friend was the only person I knew there, and when she saw me, I immediately felt welcomed. I sat in the front row with her during worship. I cheered her on during her messages. She invited me to spend time with her in the ever-elusive greenroom for speakers, and she invited me to stay and eat lunch with her and the worship team.

She didn't have to invite me in or include me, but she did anyway. I will never forget her being generous with her time, her wisdom, her space, and her very life. She opened the door and gave me access.

When I think about the word *access*, I often think of places where I am not allowed to go, places where I need a key or code to enter. Sometimes a person of influence (particularly if she is a public speaker, leader, or author) can feel inaccessible—especially when being invited usually requires having status or a connection. It can feel like only a select few have the opportunity to be on the receiving end of that person's individualized attention.

Because we are all given a measure of influence by God, we can choose whom we influence and how we do it. We hold the keys to give it away generously or to hold it high so no one can reach it.

Jesus gave generous access to His influence, His teachings, and His mercy. He healed many and fed thousands. He saw each individual person, calling them daughter and son. At every moment in Jesus's life, He chose to give those around Him access to Himself, His power, and His forgiveness.

We are called to live our lives in the same way. Let's be invitational and generous with whomever God brings into our lives.

—KARINA ALLEN

Describe a time when someone of influence, like Karina's friend, invited you in or when you have done that for someone who looks up to you.

_____

_____

_____

_____

In the verses leading up to today's story about the feeding of the five thousand in Mark 6, Jesus heard about the unjust death of His cousin, John the Baptist. John had lived his life testifying about Jesus, making the way for others to know that Jesus is the Savior of the world. But after being imprisoned, John was beheaded due to a regretful promise King Herod had made to his stepdaughter (see vv. 14–29). When Jesus heard the news, He went away to a remote area to be alone and to grieve, but the crowds found out where He was headed and followed Him (Matt. 14:12–13).

In the midst of His own grief and rejection (Mark 6:1–6), Jesus sees the crowds who have come a long way to find Him and has compassion on them (6:34; cf. Matt. 14:14). Imagine how exhausted He is, and yet His heart breaks at their longing for a shepherd. He's like a mother who endlessly pours herself out for her children even when she has nothing to give.

He takes the time to teach them "many things" (Mark 6:34)—feeding them abundantly with spiritual food as He is about to do with physical food. As the day turns toward late afternoon, Jesus turns to His disciples and tells them they need to feed the thousands who have gathered.

They are bewildered that Jesus would ask such an impossible task of them, but eventually they find food among the crowd—five loaves of bread and two fish. After Jesus blesses the food and the disciples begin to distribute it, the loaves and fish miraculously multiply and everyone eats their fill.

In His grief, Jesus could have said no to the crowds. He would have been completely justified to close and lock the door and put away the keys to His influence for a time. Instead His compassion for the people led to a generous overflow of His influence. Jesus hosted the crowd of thousands, graciously opening the way to life and truth, and spent time caring for their souls and stomachs.

It takes wisdom to know when to lean in and give others generous access to our influence when we're struggling ourselves. When was a time you felt you had no more to give but relied on God to give you the energy to pour into someone else?

Jesus's generosity is evident in *how* and *where* He met the people He influenced. At times during His ministry, Jesus taught in synagogues, but most of His recorded ministry was done where many would have access to Him—on hills and mountainsides, at the seashore, while walking from one town to another, and in people's homes.

> **Jesus's generosity is evident in how and where He met the people He influenced.**

And because of His intentionality, people from different socioeconomic classes, women, children, the blind, the bleeding, the demon-possessed, and even lepers were all able to access Him. Those who were pushed to the margins of society by cultural and religious standards were restored to their communities because Jesus made it possible. He held His arms open and embraced them, redeeming them with His words of forgiveness and His healing hands.

Karina wrote, "We are all given a measure of influence by God." What does it look like for you to generously give others access to your influence? If it helps, consider the way Jesus's generosity was evident in *how* and *where* He met people.

Mark 6:31 tells us that Jesus wanted to get away from the crowds for a while to rest, but the crowds wouldn't allow it. They followed Jesus and His disciples and didn't even give them time or space to eat. And yet it was from this place of emptiness that Jesus was able to feed them with abundance.

Rest is crucial when we're grieving and is a necessary part of our everyday rhythms. But we all have times and even lengthy seasons of life when rest is elusive. We might be in survival mode caring for family members or caring for our own mind and body, just trying to get from one day to the next. Or, as in Jesus's case, there might be those around us whose needs we're called to meet, so we set aside rest to be with them.

Jesus saw the crowds gathered and had compassion on them. Compassion requires us to be able to really see others, to recognize their needs and feel for them. Jesus was emotionally moved by what He saw in the people's eyes and by the vast size of the crowd that had gathered to hear from Him.

Like Karina's friend, Jesus didn't have to invite people in. He didn't have to be hospitable or allow the crowds into His personal space. He could've smiled and nodded and sent them home as the disciples suggested. But compassion opened His arms to care for the people who needed a shepherd, and though He was empty, He gave of Himself until everyone was full and satisfied.

Read Psalm 23. How does this image of God being our Shepherd show His generosity and compassion toward us?

How does Jesus's generosity give you courage to do the same with your influence?

Reflect on this prayer and make it your own today:

Lord, You are a God who sees, a God who notices and has compassion. Thank You. I pray that I would be able to hold the influence You've given me loosely—not hoarding it for a special few but offering it generously to many. As Jesus has done, so help me to do the same. Amen.

The point is this: The person who sows sparingly will also reap sparingly, and the person who sows generously will also reap generously. Each person should do as he has decided in his heart—not reluctantly or out of compulsion, since God loves a cheerful giver. And God is able to make every grace overflow to you, so that in every way, always having everything you need, you may excel in every good work.

2 Corinthians 9:6–8

I once heard God speak to me in a hotel room after a women's conference. Or at least I thought I did. I didn't hear an audible voice, but I did feel an unusual pressure in my chest as a thought grabbed hold of my mind and wouldn't let go. *I should write a book.* That was the first time I had that thought, but it wouldn't be the last.

For years I had been trying to find my way in a career that was proving to be either incredibly difficult or not right for me. (I'm still not sure which it was.) Though I didn't know it at the time, I'd eventually find my way into the world of publishing. But in that moment, in that hotel room, the idea that I could write a book that people would read seemed unlikely, if not impossible.

In the years that followed, I slowly took steps toward becoming a writer. I started a blog. I brainstormed ideas. I wrote down my thoughts and read the thoughts of others. I met other writers and became friends with them, and I even found the nerve to speak up and introduce myself to an agent here and an editor there. All along the way I thought

I was working toward one thing—but it turns out God had a different plan in mind.

Someday I might write a book. But for now, my job finds me sharing other people's stories and ideas instead of my own. I've polished and formatted book proposals that turned into bestsellers, proofread and edited books, contributed to compilations, and ghostwritten books—all for other women who have heard from God.

At first I thought these projects would lead to my own progress and popularity. Instead, I've had a front-row seat to see women share the good news of the gospel through those books I quietly worked on and grow in their influence and acclaim. But while that's happened, I've seen something else that's even more incredible to me. Amazingly, God has changed my stubborn heart from being prideful to being grateful. Rather than being disappointed to see someone else's name on the spine of a book I've worked on, I'm finally able to feel satisfaction in the part I played and gratitude that God allows me to be a part of His work.

Do I still want to write a book? Maybe. Am I glad my road to publishing has been a long behind-the-scenes walk of helping others share their stories first? Definitely.

—MARY CARVER

Think about the phrase "cheerful giver." What does it teach us about how our inner motivation affects our outward actions?

Paul writes to the Corinthian church, reminding them of the commitment they had made to generously give to the Christians in Jerusalem. Their generosity had inspired others to give, and Paul, as their leader and pastor, wants to keep them accountable to what they had promised.

In our passage for today, Paul explains the principles of giving. First, just as a farmer harvests in proportion to what was sowed, if we give little, we'll receive little in return. If we give a lot, we'll receive a lot in return. Next, we give what we've already decided to give and not because of pressure. This means that we don't need to measure our generosity against someone else's offering. Last, God will generously provide for us in return.

These principles seem simple enough but often get misconstrued with selfishness. Some might read Paul's words and conclude, "I better give a lot so I can get whatever I want from God." Or they might think, "I give so much already, so why haven't I gotten what I should be getting in return?"

These approaches to giving expose the underlying self-centeredness that lives in all of us. We are called to give not because we can get something in return but out of love for God and for others. The beautiful cycle of giving is that the love we receive from God is given back and forth to one another. God provides what we need, so we can always be generous. Those on the receiving end of our generosity not only have their needs met but also respond with thanksgiving to God, giving glory to Him. And in the end, we may receive their love and prayers (1 Cor. 9:11–14). Love flows freely between God and us, and between us and others.

We love freely and give generously because God first loved us.

Even if we don't get anything in return, whether acknowledgment or love, we know that at the very core of generosity is the example of Jesus. God gave His love to us completely and at great cost, even when He knew He wouldn't receive the same measure of love in return. We love freely and give generously because He first loved us (1 John 4:19), and that is good enough.

The idea of giving without getting anything in return might grate on your nerves because of its unfairness. Whether your mind goes there or not, whether you're great at giving or not, what is God showing you about the state of your heart when it comes to generosity?

_____

_____

_____

_____

Read Matthew 6:26–34. Write a prayer of thanksgiving for the ways God has provided generously for you. If it has been a difficult season of need, write a prayer to share your frustrations, to ask for specific answers for the help you need, and to thank God for the things He's already given you.

_____

_____

_____

_____

Mary's story ends in the middle, and isn't that so encouraging? Sometimes it gives us hope to hear someone's "light at the end of the tunnel" story, but mostly we find in life that the tunnel is longer than we expected. Disappointments line the tunnel walls more often than we'd like, and even the light we anticipated seeing might look different from what we'd hoped.

It's possible that Mary may or may not write a book with her name gracing the spine, but she knows she's right where she's supposed to be for now. She feels satisfaction and gratitude for the work she's doing even though someone else is getting the credit. And therein lies the heart of a cheerful giver—one who pours out and invests herself even when the return is as simple as doing work that matters.

Second Corinthians 9:8 says, "And God is able to make every grace overflow to you, so that in every way, always having everything you need, you may excel in every good work." Mary excels at the good work she does. She offers her influence of writing and editing skills generously to those who need it, and though she may not be able to see the direct impact her words make, she knows the promise Proverbs 11:25 holds for her: "A generous person will prosper; whoever refreshes others will be refreshed" (NIV).

Though our goal in giving should never be to expect something in return, this verse does guarantee that we *will* receive blessings from God when we are generous. The form of blessing may vary, but the reward each time is God Himself—knowing Him more, receiving His love and care, being a part of His good work, and having His presence with us always.

In what areas of life or in what situations can you be generous with your influence, your presence, or your skills without expecting anything in return?

The cycle of generous influence continues when we remember that giving isn't about what we can get in return but is about freely offering what we've been freely given by God. And when that happens, generosity begets generosity. Because we have the power of Christ in us to give of ourselves without holding back, may we find ourselves more like Christ in His abundant generosity, and may we inspire others to do likewise.

Read John 12:24 and our passage for today, 2 Corinthians 9:6–8. How does the John passage inform how we ought to give generously of ourselves?

_____

_____

_____

_____

Reflect on this prayer and make it your own today:

Lord, thank You for the way You abundantly provide for us. I'm so often prone to focus on myself and want acknowledgment for my generosity. Help me to be like Jesus, who gave everything— even His life—and to courageously offer my influence to others even when there's no reward. Amen.

Don't store up for yourselves treasures on earth, where moth and rust destroy and where thieves break in and steal. But store up for yourselves treasures in heaven, where neither moth nor rust destroys, and where thieves don't break in and steal. For where your treasure is, there your heart will be also.

Matthew 6:19–21

My late husband, Ericlee, was the one who first invited me to coach track and field. We had met on a mission trip together through our church, and he knew my passion for running. He was the head coach for the track and field team at a local Christian high school, where he also taught. He wanted me to focus on coaching hurdles and middle-distance races like the ones I ran as an athlete in school. He also wanted a female influence out on the field.

I quickly agreed. I enjoyed the sport and loved pouring into young people. I loved working with the girls one-on-one, building their skills as well as their confidence. We opened the Bible together at the beginning of practices. I prayed with them before races. They asked me for relationship advice on the bus. We ate meals together and became like extended family.

Our athletes also cheered us on when Ericlee and I got engaged about a year after we started coaching together. Many of them came to our wedding. They brought us gifts when our daughters were born.

Of course, our coaching was never done for the money. Given the number of hours we devoted to training the athletes and attending track meets, the stipend came out to far less than a minimum-wage job would have offered. Coaching would not garner fame or build my platform as a writer or speaker.

Still, I loved it.

It's been more than nineteen years now since that first season coaching with Ericlee. Now our three daughters are the ones out on the track, competing in the 400 meters, the relays, and the long jump. I coach them alongside their friends.

Sometimes we scatter seeds generously and cultivate them without ever knowing if, how, or when they might bloom.

One of my joys in this present season is reconnecting with some of those athletes I coached in high school who are now working women and mamas. I have the privilege of seeing how God continues to work in their lives. I love having coffee dates with Michelle to talk about marriage and parenting. Brianna still texts me with prayer requests and questions about running shoes. Leah recently joined my Facebook running group and still chases records while pushing her two little ones in a jogging stroller. These beautiful women of influence are planting seeds and tending their own gardens now, and it is my joy to still run alongside them.

—DORINA LAZO GILMORE-YOUNG

Remembering that our influence in people's lives is like seeds we sow, how has your perspective changed, if at all, about where God has placed you in this season right now?

Whether it feels like it or not, you are where you are, with the people around you, in the community you live in, at the church you're at for a reason. It might be hard to see how seeds you sow now might bear fruit, but thankfully it's God's responsibility to make things grow. Our job is to invest our influence in others for eternal impact.

In Matthew 6:19–21, Jesus preaches about the condition of our hearts in connection to our money and possessions. He urges us not to store up treasures on earth, which will one day be thrown away or destroyed, but to store up treasures in heaven, where things last forever.

Though the passage is about wealth, the same principle applies to the way we use our influence. We can strive for accolades, recognition, and even fame here on earth, but all that will mean nothing when we stand in the presence of God at the end of our lives.

Money and accolades are good, even influential, in and of themselves. But when they become everything to us, defining the way we live and work, we know our priorities are not in the right place.

Matthew 6:21 is the litmus test to know where our priorities lie: "For where your treasure is, there your heart will be also." Where and in whom we invest ourselves, how we spend our time, and how we use our influence will reveal what we truly value—building our own kingdoms or building God's.

If you put the Matthew 6:21 litmus test to your life, what would it reveal about what you truly value?

Since we are to store up our treasures in heaven, how does having an eternal perspective—one where we understand that this life isn't the

be-all and end-all—help you prioritize the way you build or use your influence here on earth?

_____

_____

_____

_____

Dorina wrote that "we scatter seeds generously and cultivate them without ever knowing if, how, or when they might bloom." In her story, she had the privilege of watching the girls she trained on the track and in life grow up to become amazing women she still had influence with. It is truly a blessing to witness the transformation of those we invest in, and we can't help but worship God with joy when we have those opportunities.

But we may not always have the chance to witness it for ourselves. Life sometimes carries us far away from the people we spent years investing in. Other times it buries us underground, keeping us small and quiet and away from the crowds we want to influence.

We long to have the glory stories of seeing things come full circle, but it's okay if we don't. Only God sees if, how, or when the seeds we scatter take root and eventually bloom—seeds that might fall on hard ground or get choked out by weeds or stay dormant in the ground for decades.

No amount of influence with our time, our life, or our presence is wasted when it's used to build God's kingdom.

It's understandable that if we planted the seed, we want to be the one to water it and watch it grow into a mature plant that bears fruit. But when that doesn't happen, we can take heart. The investment we make now, however big or small, can have ripple effects into eternity.

So when we can't see the fruit, when ordinary seasons are more plentiful than glory moments, we can rest assured that no amount of influence with our time, our life, or our presence is wasted when it's used to build God's kingdom.

Read Matthew 6:33. How does focusing on building God's kingdom help you to be generous with your influence?

Jesus's time in ministry was short. For three years He used His influence to its full extent. He spent the most time with His twelve disciples. Despite being eyewitnesses to His divine nature, they still didn't quite understand who He was. He also spent considerable time with crowds—some who believed Him, some who were healed by Him, some who didn't know what to think about Him, and others who wanted to kill Him. People followed Him by the thousands and just as quickly left Him in droves.

And at the very end of His time in ministry, after He had been betrayed by one of the Twelve, Matthew records that "all the disciples deserted him and ran away" (26:56). Despite having given them access to His influence, His life, His love, and His power, not even the people closest to Jesus were there for Him.

If we had been there, most likely we would have thought that His life came to nothing—that all the time and energy He spent going from town to town preaching and healing was just a waste since He died in the end.

But on this side of the resurrection, we know that His death was a transformative moment for all of humanity. It wasn't the end but the means by which everything we do now has meaning for eternity.

Jesus generously gave of Himself even when He was misunderstood, underappreciated, and hated. He offered all kinds of people access to truth and life and received very little respect or trust in return. He loved us just as the Father loved Him, and that's why it was worth it for Him. May we be like Jesus, generously and courageously giving of ourselves.

Finish this sentence: *I will generously use my influence by* _____
_____.

Reflect on this prayer and make it your own today:

God, we are in awe of Your Son, Jesus, who gave all of Himself and died an innocent death at the hands of those who called themselves righteous. We know that being generous will require the courage He had, so fill us with it today. Help us to think eternally and to trust You to grow the seeds we now sow. Amen.

be intentional with your influence

One day as Jesus was walking along the shore of the
Sea of Galilee, he saw two brothers—Simon, also called
Peter, and Andrew—throwing a net into the water,
for they fished for a living. Jesus called out to them,
"Come, follow me, and I will show you how to fish for
people!" And they left their nets at once and followed
him.

Matthew 4:18-20 NLT

One of the greatest joys of my college career was being discipled by Esther. This is saying a lot, because I loved pretty much everything about college. I loved studying creative writing and living in the dorms. I soaked up mountain retreats and trips to the beach with incredible new friends. But discipleship is what left the greatest mark on my heart.

I grew up in the church but sadly never heard about discipleship. I thought *disciple* was just an archaic Bible term for Jesus's most devoted followers. I didn't know that *disciple* was also a verb—a beautiful pouring into, walking alongside, investing in. Then the students and staff I met at an on-campus ministry started talking about being discipled. They mentioned Scripture memory and personal accountability. Was this like mentorship for the Christian life? I wanted to be serious about my growing faith—sign me up!

But when I started meeting with Esther, a twenty-something staffer, I discovered that being discipled wasn't about someone making sure

I'm checking off spiritual to-do boxes. It was about someone caring for my heart.

Jesus said, "By this everyone will know that you are my disciples, if you love one another" (John 13:35). I knew His words were true when I saw them lived out in Esther's life. She loved me over coffee and while hanging out in my dorm room. She loved me by asking insightful questions and pausing long enough to really listen. She loved by inviting me to her apartment and treating me to lunch. The way she made space for my whole self and let me lean in when I cried demonstrated the kind of love that showed me a Jesus I had never known.

In time, I knew I wanted to be a discipler—to love others as Esther had loved me. I started meeting with Alyssa at the local bagel shop where we would read books together and talk. I also spent time with Mey, taking long drives, sitting on park benches, and sinking our toes in the sand. Sometimes I didn't feel qualified to disciple these women. I had so much to learn about Scripture and living the faith I professed. I didn't always know what to say or how to best guide my young friends, but I knew how to share my life, how to really see someone, how to love. And that's all Jesus asked of me.

I'm pretty sure the weeks that turned into months that led to years of sharing life left a mark on Alyssa and Mey's hearts too. What a gift to be invited to love and disciple as Jesus did!

—BECKY KEIFE

Have you ever been discipled or have you discipled someone else? If so, what was that experience like?

To be a disciple means to learn from someone, which is best done by following that person's example. Children and their caregivers are an excellent example of discipleship.

Children learn to follow by copying the behaviors and actions of their caregivers—from a simple game of peekaboo, to saying the same phrases and even mimicking the tone of voice we use with them. So much of this happens intuitively, without any formal instruction or explanation. They watch and copy whatever we do, whether we like it or not. And the more they see something, the more they do it.

Jesus invited His first disciples to learn from Him in this same way using three phrases: *Come. Follow me. I will show you.*

Come is an invitation to enter into a relationship with Jesus, to be with Him. Jesus noticed two sets of brothers—Peter and Andrew, James and John—as He walked along the shore. He called them to come and trade their way of making a living for a continuously life-giving relationship with Him.

Follow me is an invitation to intimacy in our relationship with Jesus. Following Jesus means knowing Him and being known by Him. In the three intense years that Jesus did ministry, His disciples were physically and relationally close to Him. He considered them friends (John 15:15) and spent time with them—eating meals, performing miracles, teaching the crowds, and sharing all the mundane in-between moments that aren't recorded in Scripture.

I will show you is an invitation to learn to be like Jesus and the promise that He'll guide us. The disciples got to learn at Jesus's feet all the time—having small group discussions with Him after He taught the crowds, watching Him up close when He did miracles, leading alongside Him. They got to see His humanity—His anguish, joy, anger, and sorrow—and His divinity—His resurrecting power, healing power, and authority.

Jesus extends the same invitation to us: *Come. Follow Me. I will show you.*

Read Luke 5:1–11 for a more detailed description of how Jesus called His first disciples. If you were one of them, what would be your response to Jesus's invitation and why?

While you may not find your security in boats and nets as the first disciples did, what parts of your life might be keeping you from following and learning from Jesus? It could be basing your security or identity on your job, your role in the lives of others, your financial stability, or even certain relationships.

Jesus taught and fed thousands of people on hillsides and walked through countless crowds, noticing the sick and healing them. As we learned last week, He was generous with His influence and made Himself accessible to many people during His short life on earth.

But Jesus was also intentional. He chose twelve men to be part of His inner circle (Matt. 10:1–4), and at times He had an even more intimate fellowship with just Peter, James, and John. Furthermore, John refers to himself several times in his Gospel as "the disciple whom Jesus loved," and as Jesus died on the cross, He entrusted John with caring for his mother, Mary—an incredibly moving moment that shows the closeness between John and Jesus (John 19:25–27).

Being intentional with our influence requires us to narrow our focus, our care, and our investment to only a few people, or in some seasons only one person. How much time we spend with someone, the kinds of conversations we have, the vulnerability with which we share, the openness of our lives, and the guidance we give leads to long-term impact with the people we've chosen to disciple. It's intentionality plus intimacy. It means knowing them and being known by them, and in the process coming to know God more as well.

Think about the people in your life. Does someone come to mind as you're going through today's study? Write a prayer asking God how you can start being intentional in your relationship with them.

Becky wrote that sometimes she didn't feel qualified to disciple others. Discipling someone can feel intimidating, especially when we think of it as work that only pastors do after years of education and experience. But discipleship is the command given to us all (Matt. 28:19–20). We are invited to participate in the life-changing work of discipleship, and it's not about getting our teaching correct all the time but about how we live our lives as we follow Jesus.

> The life-changing work of discipleship is not about getting our teaching correct all the time but about how we live our lives as we follow Jesus.

We don't need to have an advanced knowledge of Scripture to start investing our time and our lives with those in our circles. We can start by looking at the way Jesus lived His life and how He purposely spent time with His disciples. Perhaps His invitation to "come, follow me, and I will show you" is a call for us not only to learn from Jesus but also to disciple like He did. He will show us how to do it, so let's have courage. Let's invite others into our lives and invest in them like He did.

If God has put a specific person or group of people on your heart as you went through today's study, what are three practical ways you can invite and invest in them? (If no one came to mind, you can still use those three practical ways to pass on the love of God to someone around you.)

_____

_____

_____

_____

How does investing in others and inviting them into your life (i.e., discipleship) require courage from you?

_____

_____

_____

_____

Reflect on this prayer and make it your own today:

Lord, thank You for not only seeing the crowds but seeing each individual person—including me. You are so intentional in the way You love us, and I want to learn to do the same. Give me courage when I don't feel ready or adequate enough to disciple others. Teach me, and I will learn. Amen.

Let us hold tightly without wavering to the hope we
affirm, for God can be trusted to keep his promise.
Let us think of ways to motivate one another to acts
of love and good works. And let us not neglect our
meeting together, as some people do, but encourage
one another, especially now that the day of his return is
drawing near.

Hebrews 10:23–25 NLT

I was "raised in the church" as they say. In other words, when I was growing up, church attendance—at least twice a week—was synonymous with our commitment to the Christian faith and being a "good" Christian. As a child, it meant if I never missed a Sunday service, I was guaranteed a place in heaven. This sentiment stayed with me into young adulthood, where life offered fresh soil in which to grow. Honestly, at that point, faithful church attendance left me feeling desolate and—for lack of a better word—*blah*.

Then I noticed that a few of my peers were having a very different church experience than I was. They were enthusiastic about attending church. They did life together outside of Sunday morning meetings. I watched them cheer each other on and support each other. They seemed rooted, nourished, and confident in their growing connection to Christ and to one another. And I was being nurtured through my connection to their everyday, real-life devotion. I learned much from being immersed in their authentic, ordinary lived experiences—how they encouraged, disagreed with, and forgave one another.

I had never experienced anything like that before, and I quickly made their church my church. But before I ever walked into their Sunday morning meeting or met their sunshine-y pastor, before I was officially welcomed by greeters at the door, I had already been enveloped into their community through my friends. I had witnessed the strength of connection they had with one another and had seen them live out Christ's love and truth in real life.

I have learned since then that attending a corporate gathering with wonderful music and an inspiring sermon is good. It also can be helpful to read and follow popular Christian influencers and listen to podcasts, watch livestream conferences, and attend seminars. But being connected authentically and doing ordinary life with other folks on a Christ-centered journey fosters true, mutual discipleship. I get to glean from others' life experiences and wisdom, and they get to learn from mine. Together we learn from God and see a fuller picture of Him through each other. In connection and community, we get to stir one another to love well and do good works.

—LUCRETIA BERRY

What role have relationships played in your experience of church (either when you were growing up or in your current life stage)?

_____

_____

_____

_____

The meaning of church, community, and discipleship in our technological age is so unlike past eras, when physical gatherings were the only kind of connection believers had with one another. Now we have services streamed online, and pastors write books and host podcasts. We have churches that only meet online and others that have multiple campuses around the city. There are small groups and Bible study groups within the church and outside of the church, and a plethora of resources are available to us at the click of a button.

We live in an amazing time when we have access to more knowledge than we can possibly consume and more opportunities than ever before to connect online and in person. And yet loneliness is pervasive and discipleship is lacking.[1] Those who live Bible-centered lives are still a small percent of the Christian population, which tells us that while we say we believe, we don't have a good foundation for our faith nor do we put our faith into practice in transformative ways.[2]

The discrepancy of having access to too much but consuming the wrong things for spiritual nourishment has created bloated believers—those who profess faith in Jesus and consume Christian knowledge through books, podcasts, sermons, and conferences, but who are not changed by it. And because of that, their lives don't influence others toward faith in Jesus.

We need more than just attending services on Sunday or being connected to one another on social media. We need an authentic community committed to intentionally living out the faith we profess.

Do you think you have a good foundation of faith—both in orthodoxy (what you believe) and orthopraxy (how you practice your beliefs)? How does having a weak orthodoxy and orthopraxy affect the kind of influence you can have on others?

Read Acts 2:42–47 and Hebrews 10:23–25. How did the early church actively live out their faith?

_____

_____

_____

_____

The early church we see in Acts 2:42–47 is minimalist compared with what we see in churches today, which are often run by a calendar of events—Christmas programs, Easter celebrations, and summer camps, with prayer meetings sprinkled throughout. Each of those things can be life-giving and helpful for church vitality, but discipleship happens most effectively through relationships with one another on the ground level, not through events or programs.

Lucretia was affected less by the routine of tradition and more by what she saw in regular moments with her friends—how they disagreed and forgave, how they cheered each other on, and how they were devoted in their everyday life. They did what the author of Hebrews urges us to do, and it changed Lucretia's life.

We need community alongside us to help us persevere when we feel like we can't go any further and to bring us back to the center of the road when we start to veer off too much to one side or the other. With our individualist mentality in Western culture, we too often think it's enough to have a "personal" faith that's just between Jesus and me, but faith is both personal and communal. We were made as part of a body—the body of Christ.

Living authentically with one another means choosing community over self again and again.

In our current culture of faux connection, it will take extra intentionality for us to live authentically with one another. It will mean choosing community over self again and again. It will mean leaning in toward someone when it would be more comfortable to back away. It will mean courageously being our whole selves with no facade, knowing we'll mess up from time to time but that it's okay. We can repent when we've done wrong, ask for forgiveness when necessary, and still be in relationship with our community.[3]

> **What are some ways you can intentionally pursue deeper connections with the church/faith community you're in? If you don't have one yet, what are some barriers keeping you from being part of one?**

_____

_____

_____

_____

Being intentional with our influence goes against the trend of shallow discipleship in the church. It means we do the three "let us" statements in Hebrews 10:23–25:

Let us hold tightly to the hope we affirm.

Let us think of ways to motivate one another to acts of love and good works.

Let us not neglect our meeting together but encourage one another.

We must live out the faith we profess—loving and serving others, being merciful and forgiving, working toward justice and reconciliation, *and* growing in our knowledge of God. We must commit to being communal in our faith—sharing the love of Jesus through the way we live, inviting others into genuine truth-telling relationships, and meeting together regularly to keep motivating one another.

We all long for this in the church, and it can happen. It starts by being intentional with how we live out what we believe so that others are changed as well.

Read Hebrews 10:23–25 in *The Message*. What stands out to you in this version compared with the New Living Translation we read at the beginning of our study today?

Reflect on this prayer and make it your own today:

God, I'm so grateful we don't have to do this faith journey alone. For those of us who don't have a community to call family, I ask that You will provide one. Give me the courage to lean into authenticity, to be intentional in encouraging others toward love and good works as I eagerly await Christ's return. Amen.

Now that same day two of them were on their way
to a village called Emmaus, which was about seven
miles from Jerusalem. Together they were discussing
everything that had taken place. And while they were
discussing and arguing, Jesus himself came near and
began to walk along with them.

Luke 24:13–15

I sat across the table from her at a local Chinese restaurant, strangers eager to get to know each other. I was the new associate pastor on staff, and though it wasn't part of my job description to meet with the young adults in our congregation, she seemed hungry for connection and care.

Over shared plates of noodles and savory meats, I asked about her life and what it was like growing up at the church. She opened up about her family, how she had been raised by a single parent, and the hurts—even traumas—she had received from pastors and fellow youth group students in the past. She didn't know how to feel about church, but she was curious and perhaps even a tinge hopeful that things could be different with the younger pastors who had come on board recently.

I met with her and many others over the first year of my time on staff, trying to get a pulse for what God was doing, what the ministry and the congregation needed, and how I was to invest in the people who were hungry and ready to be discipled.

I was new to ministry and had seen leaders of the church I grew up in only use programs and curriculum they found in mainstream ministries to "do" discipleship. But those didn't fit the culture of our city and the people who were in our community, so I did what I knew how to do: feed people and create a safe place for them to be.

Once my husband and I were ready to buy a home, we discussed what we wanted most out of it, and we both agreed that the most important thing would be an open space where people could gather comfortably. We imagined hosting small groups and movie nights, Friendsgivings and Christmas parties, and when we did find the right house, that's exactly what we got to do. But more than those big get-togethers, I realize now that discipleship happened most at our dinner table.

Food was always a sure way to ease into conversations where I could share what I saw God doing in someone's life, guide them when they needed it, and be there for them when they ached for a place to belong. I walked with them through family issues, church frustrations, and relationship sorrows and joys. I didn't follow a program or even read books together with them, but it was at the dinner table that our eyes were opened to see God.

—GRACE P. CHO

What did you learn about discipleship in the church, and how has it been modeled for you?

_____

_____

_____

_____

The story in Luke 24:13–15 about the two disciples walking to Emmaus is such a clear picture of what discipleship looks like.

On the day Jesus rose from the dead, the women in His life came to the tomb and found the stone rolled away and His body gone. An angel told them He had risen, just as He said He would, and they rushed to tell the disciples. Unfortunately, the disciples didn't believe the women and wondered what had happened to Jesus.

The two men on the road to Emmaus are confused and grieving. The person they had followed for the last three years had been killed, and now what were they to do? We can imagine them questioning everything that had transpired when Jesus was alive, trying to piece together what was true, what wasn't, and what was the whole point of it all.

In the midst of their deep discussion, Jesus comes near and starts to walk alongside them. Isn't that exactly what we desire when we're in the midst of grief and confusion? When we don't know what to do and need someone to help us? Jesus comes along and walks with them. He is present in their grief and opens the conversation for them to share with Him: "What is this dispute that you're having with each other as you are walking?" (Luke 24:17). As Jesus had often done in His ministry, He asks a question to give them the opportunity to share what's on their hearts and minds.

Flabbergasted, they give a brief summary of what had just happened with the empty tomb, and Jesus begins to tell them the story of Himself once again. They don't recognize Him until later, but when they do, they exclaim, "Weren't our hearts burning within us while he was talking to us on the road and explaining the Scriptures to us?" (24:32).

Discipleship, then, is coming alongside one another, sharing life and its struggles, and pointing one another to Jesus—our Hope, our Answer, and our God. He showed us the way on the road to Emmaus, and we can follow in His footsteps.

Read the Scripture for today in context (Luke 24:13–34). Imagine yourself in the shoes of those two followers. How would it feel to recognize Jesus in your midst while grieving His death and

"disappearance"? From the story, what encourages you about who Jesus is?

_____

_____

_____

_____

The two followers recognize Jesus when He takes the bread at the meal, asks for God's blessing on it, and breaks it for them to eat together. What other meal does this breaking of bread remind you of? (Hint: see Luke 22:19–20.)

_____

_____

_____

_____

Food and discipleship are deeply connected. During Jesus's ministry, He turned water into wine (John 2:1–10) and fed more than five thousand people with bread and fish (Luke 9:10–17). He ate with tax collectors (Luke 5:27–30) and at the home of His friends Martha, Mary, and Lazarus (Luke 10:38–42). He broke bread with His disciples at the Last Supper (Luke 22:7–30), symbolizing His coming death, and twice He ate with them after His resurrection (see Luke 24:41–42 and John 21:1–13).

Food brings people together. The table naturally lends itself to community and sharing. When we gather for a meal with friends, we can relax and rest in their company. We enjoy delicious food made by the hands of those who love us, and conversation flows easily. The environment is filled with joy and laughter, and when we leave for home, we're filled to the brim in so many ways.

We can be intentional with our influence by creating space for it at the table. In doing so, we will disciple others holistically—nourishing their body, mind, and soul.

> **We can be intentional with our influence by creating space for it at the table.**

As you consider who you could invest in, it might feel intimidating to know how to start the conversation. Write down some questions you could use to help get the conversation going. For example, what has God been showing you lately about Himself?

_____

_____

_____

_____

The two followers on the road to Emmaus recognize Jesus when He blesses and breaks the bread. Could they have been there when He did the same at the feeding of the five thousand (Luke 9:10–17)? On the very day He rises from the dead, Jesus communes with them over bread—a picture of what communion means for us today.

In church, we practice the sacrament of communion to remember Jesus's death on the cross. In Luke 22:19, He tells His disciples, "This is my body, which is given for you. Do this in remembrance of me." When we tear off a piece of bread or take the wafer from the communion plate, we recognize that we can commune with God and be in community with one another because Jesus's body was broken for us.

So every time we intentionally gather at the table, it's a picture of communion. When we bless the food, break it apart, and eat it, may we be aware of Jesus's presence and see Him in one another's lives.

If food isn't your thing, what other activities can you do together with people you want to disciple?

Reflect on this prayer and make it your own today:

Father, thank You for the beautiful picture of discipleship through this story in Luke 24. I want to intentionally invest in others as Jesus did. Help me to remember the simplicity and urgency of discipling others so that You can be made known inside and outside of the church. Amen.

Jesus came near and said to them, "All authority has been given to me in heaven and on earth. Go, therefore, and make disciples of all nations, baptizing them in the name of the Father and of the Son and of the Holy Spirit, teaching them to observe everything I have commanded you. And remember, I am with you always, to the end of the age."

Matthew 28:18–20

Sitting in a women's conference and hearing the speaker urge us to make discipleship our focus, I felt my shoulders slump as I sighed. It seemed I couldn't go anywhere without hearing another Christian leader tell me I needed to be making disciples.

For years I'd struggled to find my place—both literally and figuratively. Convinced I was called to do something "big" for God, I looked for places where I could travel or relocate, certain I couldn't serve Him just a few miles from where I grew up. Overwhelmed by the emphasis on discipleship (both from my church as well as from other ministries) but misunderstanding what discipleship meant, I felt like a failure.

After all, I hadn't baptized anyone. I hadn't trained anyone to replace me as a small group leader. I wasn't going into all the nations, and I certainly wasn't sharing the gospel with thousands. I just tried to actively care for a few people in my life—a friend, a former coworker, a neighbor. As it turns out, that's actually the definition of discipleship.

While to some God said, "Go, therefore, and travel to foreign lands," or "Go, therefore, and teach the masses," His call for me has been different. I've heard Him whisper, "Go, therefore, and . . .

. . . text a friend to check in."

. . . drop off groceries when she has the flu (even though she says she's fine)."

. . . invite your divorced friend and her kids to your Thanksgiving dinner."

. . . take the neighbor along on your family field trip."

. . . meet that friend for lunch, even when your to-do list is too long."

. . . remind her, again, that she is loved even if she still hasn't come back to church."

God has placed a small number of people on my heart and asked me to be there for them. Not a single one of them goes to my church or attends my small group. I don't see them on Sundays, and more often than not our conversations are about things other than faith. Still, I smile now when I hear someone speak about discipleship, sighing in relief instead of shame. God has called us all to make disciples, but His plan for how we do that is unique to each one of us. And rather than feeling defeated, I'm finally ready to go, therefore, and be exactly who He made me to be.

—MARY CARVER

If you were familiar with the Great Commission in Matthew 28:18–20 before now, how have you heard it explained or what was your understanding of it?

_____

_____

_____

_____

In the penultimate scene of Jesus's earthly life, He commissions His disciples with a final word: go and make disciples. It's an empowering moment for the disciples right before Jesus ascends to heaven, but it's prefaced with a mixture of emotions. Matthew 28:17 tells us that they worshiped Him but some still doubted. And who can blame them? They had gone through a whirlwind of tragic and glorious events—the betrayal of their Friend and Teacher, His death, the amazing yet confusing resurrection that followed three days later, and then seeing Him in the flesh several times before this moment. We can understand the disbelief that lingered in them.

To this tender, unsure group of followers, Jesus declares that He has been given all authority in heaven and on earth. With this complete power, He anoints them to go and make disciples with the same authority.

Doubt is replaced with authority, and we see a glimpse of it at the end of Mark's Gospel, where he tells us, "So the Lord Jesus, after speaking to them, was taken up into heaven and sat down at the right hand of God. And they went out and preached everywhere, while the Lord worked with them and confirmed the word by the accompanying signs" (16:19–20).

Doubt doesn't prevent us from receiving the authority God gives us through Christ. The guarantee is that we who believe in Him will be given power through Jesus.

Therefore, it's in His name that we have the authority and responsibility to disciple others. It's not only up to pastors and other leaders in the church. It is our commission from God Himself to teach and walk alongside people in knowing and becoming like Jesus.

Mark 1:22 tells us that, unlike the other religious teachers, Jesus spoke with authority. Knowing that you have the same authority in you because of Christ, how does it change the way you view your authority to disciple others?

Some sermons about the Great Commission teach that making disciples of all nations means going overseas *to* all the nations. This message has inspired many to become missionaries who are sent out from their country of origin to various locations around the globe. And though this is a worthy cause, we have mistakenly understood the Great Commission to be only that.

Making disciples of all people means also doing that right where we're at. Like Mary wrote, it can be showing up and loving the people we see on a weekly basis—the friend who's sick, the neighbor who doesn't have a family, the church member who left and hasn't returned. It can be joining an organization that helps the most marginalized in our communities—those who are disabled, who don't have homes, who are being abused and neglected. It can be the persevering work of loving family members who are adamantly against your faith and mock you for it, or it can be the long-haul fight for justice in broken legal systems. It can be done whether you're traveling around the globe or bedridden with an autoimmune disease.

The point is to intentionally make disciples—not converts—who believe *and* do what we ourselves have learned. This happens through relationships and time spent walking alongside each other. Unfortunately, we have too often counted and rejoiced over the number of converts who have raised their hands at rallies while lacking the follow-up discipleship that teaches them to live out everything Jesus has commanded us to do.

Walk with the people who are right around you—whether that's in your neighborhood or in a country on the other side of the world.

Walk with the people who are right around you—whether that's in your neighborhood or in a country on the other side of the world. Wherever you are, whatever capacity you have, the Great Commission applies to you.

List three ways you can live out the Great Commission in your local community and three ways you can do it on a larger or even global scale.

_____

_____

_____

_____

In today's opening thoughts, Mary felt unsure whether she knew how to do discipleship. The disciples doubted even as they saw the resurrected Jesus in front of them. We might feel similarly. If so, let Jesus's final words be comforting and empowering for you: "And remember, I am with you always, to the end of the age" (Matt. 28:20).

This is the promise of the ultimate Discipler. He who walked alongside His disciples, patiently teaching them and breaking bread with them, does the same for us. The promise comes with a double guarantee at the end—"always, to the end of the age." We are assured that we can live out the Great Commission, even when it feels like an overwhelming commandment.

When Jesus was born, the word of the prophet Isaiah was fulfilled: He was Immanuel—God with us (Matt. 1:23; cf. Isa. 7:14). That name continues to be true even after Jesus ascended to heaven. Now He is with us through the Holy Spirit who lives _within_ us, and He will continue to be with us till the very end of the age.

How does living out the Great Commission wherever you are require you to be courageous?

_____

_____

Reflect on this prayer and make it your own today:

God, You have given me the authority to go and make disciples—even when I doubt and feel unqualified. Help me to see discipleship with new eyes and to have courage to love those around me, to be part of Your work of redemption and restoration in the world, and to do it with the authority You have anointed me with through Jesus. Amen.

Remain in me, and I in you. Just as a branch is unable
to produce fruit by itself unless it remains on the vine,
neither can you unless you remain in me. I am the vine;
you are the branches. The one who remains in me
and I in him produces much fruit, because you can do
nothing without me. If anyone does not remain in me,
he is thrown aside like a branch and he withers. They
gather them, throw them into the fire, and they are
burned. If you remain in me and my words remain in
you, ask whatever you want and it will be done for you.
My Father is glorified by this: that you produce much
fruit and prove to be my disciples.

John 15:4–8

Out of the corner of my eye, I noticed Katharina. She was a woman in my soul care workshop at church who was rather quiet and didn't interact much with others at her table.

My workshops are interactive, and one activity I guide everyone through is watercolor prayers. We paint to express a Scripture that has spoken to us. This woman painted a beautiful peony flower, but when I asked her to share, she was very shy.

After class, I thought I'd say hello and try to talk to her, but her quietness made me wonder if I was asking her too many questions instead of letting her have her own space.

As I drove home that day, I became worried and self-conscious that I had tried too hard to make conversation happen with her. I could hear my mother's voice in my head telling me that I talk too much. I was a very outgoing girl as a child, but the message I kept hearing from her was that it would be better if I stayed quiet.

Maybe that's why I'm drawn to those who tend to shy away from conversations. I enjoy befriending them and helping them come out of their shells. As I reflected on this childhood memory, I felt God gently whisper to my soul, "You have My words." That simple phrase kept repeating in my heart.

The next week, I decided to ask this new friend out for dinner. I was nervous and wondered if she only felt obligated to say yes because I was the workshop speaker for the class.

But in the end, dinner was enjoyable and we talked for hours, leaving only when the restaurant was about to close.

Two years later, Katharina texted me to share how my gentleness in our friendship meant so much to her. I was only being who I naturally am, but to my friend, that was the exact influence she needed me to be at that time.

—BONNIE GRAY

How have you influenced someone just by being who you naturally are?

All week we've talked about being intentional with our influence, and though we should be thoughtful and purposeful with it, our Scripture passage today tells us that we also bear fruit just by abiding in Jesus, the Vine.

He says in John 15:5, "I am the vine; you are the branches. The one who *remains* in me and I in him produces much fruit." Remaining sounds passive—like something we do by inaction. But if we read further, we see what Jesus means by remaining. "If you keep my commands, you will remain in my love, just as I have kept my Father's commands and remain in his love" (v. 10).

Staying connected to the Vine means that we obey His commands. Obeying means responding to His love by doing what He asks of us, because our relationship with God goes both ways. There is receiving and giving. He loves us, and we love Him in return. He remains in us through the Holy Spirit, and we remain in Him by actively walking in obedience.

If we want to bear fruit, we must remain in the Vine, and therefore our greatest efforts to be intentional must first go to abiding in Christ.

Bonnie didn't do anything out of the ordinary when she first met Katharina. Out of her abundant love for God and others, she paid attention to how Katharina responded and made space for her quietness. She had learned to do that through the pain she had experienced in her own life, but it bore in her a tenderness that helps her see and care for people.

Her staying connected to the Vine produced a friendship in which Katharina saw God's kindness to her through Bonnie.

Read Galatians 5:22–25. What fruit do you see being born in you or through you?

_____

_____

_____

_____

173

Unfortunately, it is all too easy to look like we're remaining in the Vine when we aren't. We can do all the outward practices that appear as though God's love is bearing fruit in us, but without God's love in us, it's all for nothing. The apostle Paul talks about this in 1 Corinthians 13:

> If I speak human or angelic tongues but do not have love, I am a noisy gong or a clanging cymbal. If I have the gift of prophecy and understand all mysteries and all knowledge, and if I have all faith so that I can move mountains but do not have love, I am nothing. And if I give away all my possessions, and if I give over my body in order to boast but do not have love, I gain nothing. (vv. 1–3)

Actions without love ring hollow, and if we are simply striving to appear loving, we eventually run out of steam and are left feeling resentful and burned out. We cannot bear true fruit without being connected to the Vine, and fake fruit will be made obvious sooner rather than later. For example, if we took store-bought apples and tried to glue them onto some bare branches so the tree looks nice, they might look ripe and beautiful from a distance. It won't be long, however, before the apples rot and fall off, exposing the branches for what they really are—unfruitful.

Likewise, we can attend multiple small groups each week or post daily Bible verses on our Instagram accounts, but if we aren't spending actual time with the Lord in prayer, our professed faith will eventually reveal itself to be as unfruitful as the branches with glued-on apples.

This is a warning for us to make sure we are connected to Christ. When we are not abiding in Him, it will eventually show through our lack of love and Christlikeness.

Read John 15:2. Why is it necessary to be pruned in order to stay connected to the Vine?

Every tree and plant needs to be pruned to increase its fruitfulness. The most delicious fruits often take years to produce, and pruning is necessary before that can happen.

Pruning is intentionally removing branches from a tree or vine in order to promote stronger and guided growth to happen. God intentionally prunes us *for our sake.*

God is our Gardener (John 15:1), and He does not leave us on our own. He invests time in caring for each of us. Anyone who has had a houseplant knows that it requires routine tending. We have to inspect the leaves, check the soil, feed it fertilizer, water it at the right time, give it enough sunlight, and prune when and where necessary.

And God does the same for us. Pruning is done out of love so that we can bear even more fruit. Pruning happens through community, life circumstances, and God's Word illuminated to us.

> **Influence starts with staying connected to the Vine.**

As we learn to be intentional with our influence, we must remember that it starts with staying connected to the Vine and letting God our Gardener do His good work in us so that we will bear much fruit.

How does God's intentional care for us inspire you to be intentional with others?

Reflect on this prayer and make it your own today:

God, thank You for being a Gardener who so lovingly tends to Your children. You prune and guide my growth without fail, and I can trust You to care for me. As You have been intentional with me, help me to be intentional with others, and may my life bear fruit that will last. Amen.

tell your story

Now many Samaritans from that town believed in him because of what the woman said when she testified, "He told me everything I ever did." So when the Samaritans came to him, they asked him to stay with them, and he stayed there two days. Many more believed because of what he said. And they told the woman, "We no longer believe because of what you said, since we have heard for ourselves and know that this really is the Savior of the world."

John 4:39–42

I'm lonely, God, and I could really use a reminder that somehow, some way, it's all going to be okay.

Halfway through a twelve-hour solo drive back home, I spoke those words into the silence of my car and waited. The previous three months held joy, laughter, and delight. But they held sadness and loss too. Our days rarely involve just one emotion, and the long drive provided plenty of time to think, process, and pray.

As I glanced out the window to my left, I saw one small bird flying alone.

Well, that feels about right, I thought.

But then, half a mile farther down the road, something caught my eye. A small flock of birds joined the one, ten sets of wings flapping in unison.

A thought began to run through my mind like the news ticker that scrolls along the bottom of the television screen.

Daughter, I love you this much and more. As far as these birds go, My love goes on even farther for you.

The pavement stretched ahead and the birds flew just above, and as I leaned forward to watch them lead the way, my jaw dropped as I blinked furiously, hardly able to comprehend the sight in front of me.

Out of nowhere, more birds came together and flew in a *V* formation in front of my car. I stretched farther, straining to see where they ended, but I simply couldn't find it. On and on and on they flew, hundreds suddenly gathered together.

I don't know whether the drivers and passengers in the cars beside me noticed the birds that day, but the moment marked me. Nearly a decade has passed since that long drive home, but the birds continue to come.

In fact, I'm writing these words while sitting outside, and as I put a period on the end of that sentence, a small gray bird came and perched on the signpost just a few feet to my right.

God's love goes on and on and on. The words are simple, but the reality of the promise is life-changing. We aren't flying or driving or walking alone. He is here, with us even now.

The kingdom of God is breaking through in a million little ways.

—**KAITLYN BOUCHILLON**

Think about the stories you've heard in your life. What were some of the most powerful ones that helped you see God?

_____

_____

_____

_____

When we tell our stories, we can have influence far and wide. Because our stories live through their retelling, they can continue to inspire and encourage others over time and place.

When we tell a story of what God has done in our lives, we invite others in to share our current seasons, our pains, and our joys. Stories enable them to step into our shoes and see what we see, learn what we've learned, and perhaps have their own aha moment as well.

There's a reason why Jesus often spoke in parables to teach truth. When someone starts to lecture or preach at us, we tend to tune out. But stories invite our ears to stay open, our hearts to be moved, and our souls to be transformed.

The Samaritan woman's interaction with Jesus changes her life. He approaches her by asking for a drink of water, but in their conversation He reveals to her that He knows her. He understands her broken relationships and her thirst for something or someone to fill her longing.

She is known—not to be condemned but to be loved—and she is transformed by this.

She goes to her village and tells her community, "He told me everything I ever did" (John 4:39). Her testimony about this God-moment that changed her life ends up affecting her whole community. They believe Jesus "really is the Savior of the world" (v. 42) because she told them her story.

We all have stories to tell—stories that can lift the veil for others so they too can see God for themselves. Let's remember the God-moments in our lives and consider how we can tell our stories with courage.

Read Psalm 66:16. Why do you think God places such priority on us telling our stories?

Kaitlyn saw God through nature, specifically in the birds. How does God seem to speak to you? Aside from nature, other examples could include books, movies, interactions with people, church, the Bible, or food.

_____

_____

_____

_____

The ancient Celtic Christians used the term "thin place" to describe locations that have an ethereal quality where they believed that heaven and earth actually came together.[1]

The term "thin place" could also be used to describe those moments when the kingdom of God breaks through and God's presence seems almost tangible. It could be through the most ordinary things—like the way the wind blows through our hair or how raindrops fall a certain way down the window—or it could be a miracle of healing or provision that could only happen supernaturally.

When the kingdom of God breaks through in these ways, it clarifies. We see God for who He is—almighty, good, and beautiful—and we see ourselves and our circumstances rightly as well.

God wants us to know we are loved and known by Him, as the Samaritan woman and Kaitlyn both felt. When we share these stories of "thin place" moments, we show others a God who cares, a God who is near and who doesn't hold us at a distance. Our storytelling evokes a longing for God in them too, and it creates an opening for us to share even more.

Do you have a story like Kaitlyn's where God showed up and spoke powerfully to you through something ordinary? When you think about the stories God has written in your life thus far, do you see any themes or patterns?

_____

_____

_____

_____

From the beginning of time, God started writing a story. It's a story of love, heartache, longing, and redemption. There's action and romance, songs and history, prophecy and proverbs. Some parts can be confusing, and people interpret passages in different ways.

The very last verse in the Gospel of John says, "And there are also many other things that Jesus did, which, if every one of them were written down, I suppose not even the world itself could contain the books that would be written" (21:25). We don't know every story from Jesus's life, but God continues His story through our lives. He weaves truth through our stories, and He isn't done yet. As long as we are living, He is writing, and our stories hold power to change the world and affect those who hear them to turn toward God.

Each of our stories is unique to us, and they are *our* stories to tell, not anyone else's. We don't need to compare our testimony with someone else's to see whose is better or cooler. God wants us to tell our stories through our specific lenses, in our voices, and by our written words. And that takes courage.

> **Each of our stories is unique to us, and they are our stories to tell, not anyone else's.**

Storytelling is vulnerable, and some stories will be harder to share because of the amount of pain attached to them. However, it might be through those very stories that God wants to bring healing to others.

Let's remember what God has done in our lives and start to write our stories down. Perhaps we will fill books that the whole world cannot contain to show them Jesus.

As you reflect on the stories God has written in your life, what perspectives are unique to you? For example, it could be growing up overseas, being biracial, or living with an unseen disability.

_____

_____

_____

_____

Read Jeremiah 1:8–9. How does this Scripture give you courage to tell your story, even when it might be vulnerable and painful?

_____

_____

_____

_____

Reflect on this prayer and make it your own today:

God, You write the best stories. Thank You for wanting to share Yourself through the ones You've written in my life. Help me remember the moments when Your presence felt so near and how You have been faithful for all these years, and as I recount them to others, I pray that it would turn hearts toward You. Amen.

When Jesus came by, he looked up at Zacchaeus and called him by name. "Zacchaeus!" he said. "Quick, come down! I must be a guest in your home today."

Zacchaeus quickly climbed down and took Jesus to his house in great excitement and joy. But the people were displeased. "He has gone to be the guest of a notorious sinner," they grumbled.

Meanwhile, Zacchaeus stood before the LORD and said, "I will give half my wealth to the poor, LORD, and if I have cheated people on their taxes, I will give them back four times as much!"

Jesus responded, "Salvation has come to this home today, for this man has shown himself to be a true son of Abraham. For the Son of Man came to seek and save those who are lost."

Luke 19:5–10 NLT

I was in a season of waiting.

We were preparing for a move from central California to the mountains of Haiti to direct a nonprofit there. We were waiting for our home to sell and for the long list of details to fall into place.

My heart felt barren. We anticipated saying hard goodbyes to our beloved friends and family, but I never knew when that time would come. I was in a strange holding pattern—impatient and unsure of what to feel or what the next right step would be.

One blustery February day, my doorbell rang. I opened the door and there on my porch saw a gift tied with a periwinkle ribbon. It was a book—*One Thousand Gifts* by Ann Voskamp.

That gift from my friend showed up right on time. In the weeks to follow, I learned the powerful art of gratitude. Ann challenges her readers to make a daily practice of counting gifts, and there in those mundane days, God began to train my heart for the future. He began to show me His glory in ordinary moments.

While I waited, I started a gratitude journal. I thanked God for the laughter ringing out in our halls, the warm hug of a knitted sweater, the candy sweetness of strawberries, and the extra time at our table with friends. I savored evening runs and sunset colors waltzing across the sky. I even learned to thank Him for the leaky roof and the bare pantry shelves.

God also used my two young daughters to teach me about gratitude. I learned to thank Him for the sound of a chair scraping across the kitchen floor and a little girl offering to "help" her mama with dinner. Instead of rolling my eyes with impatience, I jotted down my gratefulness for sticky-face kisses, a whole bag of chips dumped on the floor (which gave me an excuse to sweep), and hours in the glider chair nursing my youngest.

My gratitude list spread across the years. I was deeply grateful for friends who bravely stood with me at the grave when I buried my husband, for the words of blessing a mentor prayed over me, and for a local church that collected funds to help pay our medical bills. All of these reminded me that I was not alone, that God saw me and loved me personally. He showed up again and again in these little gifts.

—DORINA LAZO GILMORE-YOUNG

How has God shown up in your life through the little things? How have you felt seen by Him?

_____

_____

Zacchaeus was a chief tax collector, someone who was despised by the Jews. Tax collectors worked for the Roman government (the ruling power at the time), and they would overtax people to keep the extra for themselves (Luke 3:13). Luke 19:2 tells us that Zacchaeus "had become very rich" (NLT), which he had done at the expense of the people in his region.

On this day Jesus comes to his town, and Zacchaeus, eager to get a look at Jesus, tries to see over the crowd but can't—he's too short. But that doesn't stop him. He runs on ahead and climbs a tree so he can wait and watch from there.

Zacchaeus is a grown man, but he seems like a child in this story—eager, curious, and too short.

Jesus comes by, looks up at him in the tree, and calls him by name: "Zacchaeus! Quick, come down! I must be a guest in your home today" (Luke 19:5 NLT). Zacchaeus only wanted to get a glimpse of the Man he heard so many people talking about, but instead Jesus offers him abundantly more: Jesus sees him and calls him by name and invites him into a new life in Him.

When we think of the testimonies we hear in church or at retreats, the ones that seem to have the most impact on people are those with a dramatic before-and-after story. We want evidence of transformation and a triumphant ending. Those stories are powerful, but we need all kinds of testimonies to see more of God.

> **We need stories of when God showed up in little ways as much as in the miraculous.**

We need to hear the stories where change happened slowly but surely. We need stories of when God showed up in little ways as much as in the miraculous. We need to know that God is present in the quiet small moments as much as He is in the more obvious ones.

Zacchaeus's story has both, but it all started because Jesus looked up and saw him.

What are some of the key moments in your own faith journey?

The story of Zacchaeus has some similarities to the story of Mary Magdalene's encounter with Jesus after His resurrection. Read Luke 19:1–5 and John 20:11–16. What similarities do you see in the two stories?

Our names are intricately tied to our identities, and we feel known when someone calls us by our name. Even though Zacchaeus is hiding in a tree and is probably despised by many in the crowd, Jesus sees him. And not only does He see him but He chooses to be his guest.

We cannot fathom the reach of God's grace and whom it will touch. Being seen by Jesus immediately affected not only Zacchaeus's life but also the lives of the people he had extorted. Luke 19:8 says, "Meanwhile, Zacchaeus stood before the Lord and said, 'I will give half my wealth to the poor, Lord, and if I have cheated people on their taxes, I will give them back four times as much!'" (NLT).

Zacchaeus's testimony isn't simply about him giving money back to those he had wronged, however. The glory moment was in being seen.

Imagine God finding you in the crowd, looking you straight in the face, and saying, "I see you. I know you. I love you." How does that make you feel, and how would you respond to Him?

Dorina's story of gratitude shows us that glory happens more often in the mundane. She paid attention to how God was showing up in the little things—the gift on her doorstep, the extra time with friends, the "help" from her daughter, and the beauty of nature. In doing so, she recognized that God's glory is all around, that His presence is always with her—through the waiting and even through her husband's death.

Our stories tell others they are not alone. We all want to be seen and known—even those who, like Zacchaeus, may have wronged others. We are like children longing for attention from someone who loves us for who we are, who knows us, and who wants to be with us.

Perhaps that's why we ought to share more stories of seeing God in the little things, because then others will know to look for Him there too. It's still true that God shows up in highlight-reel moments, but when we long for hope in difficult seasons, we want to know God is there even when there's nothing great to show for it.

Let's not measure our God-stories by their wow factor, and let's not hesitate to tell of our ordinary moments for fear that they're not good enough. Let's remember that wherever God's presence is, there is His glory—even in the mundane.

Read Psalm 9:1–2 and then write down at least five things—big or small—you are grateful for.

Reflect on this prayer and make it your own today:

Lord, thank You for seeing me and calling me by name. Thank You that Your presence is all that I need in the everyday moments of life, particularly in the moments that are invisible to others. You are real, You are near, and You are good. Help me to pay attention to the little ways You show up in my life and to share those joyfully with others. Amen.

Listen, Israel: The LORD our God, the LORD is one. Love the LORD your God with all your heart, with all your soul, and with all your strength. These words that I am giving you today are to be in your heart. Repeat them to your children. Talk about them when you sit in your house and when you walk along the road, when you lie down and when you get up. Bind them as a sign on your hand and let them be a symbol on your forehead. Write them on the doorposts of your house and on your city gates.

Deuteronomy 6:4–9

I can't count the number of times I've told this story. Each time I tell it, tears well in my eyes. I was in London, England, on a college internship, spending six weeks learning how to be a journalist.

One Sunday, about two weeks into my time there, I went to an Ethiopian church. It was old and beautiful. London was in the midst of a heat wave that summer; I can still feel the sweat clinging to the nape of my neck.

I'd been asking God to reveal why He brought me to England. I knew I was there for an internship, but I felt like God had me there for a distinct reason. For the past two weeks I'd been curious, trying to uncover what that reason might be.

The worship band played a song I didn't know. I listened to the words, letting them softly land in my heart. I stood in the pew, hot and sweating, and I began to pray.

"Why did You bring me to London?" I asked God silently.

I remember as a little girl thinking that real romance would be if a guy flew somewhere to tell me he loved me. For some reason, I felt like a sweeping gesture of that magnitude would mean everything. I'd never shared that thought with anyone—including God—because it felt vulnerable and childish. Instead I kept it a secret tucked away in my heart.

In that church, I pressed my palms against the wooden pew and continued to pray. "Why am I here?"

I did not hear an audible voice, but I felt God speaking to me quietly and tenderly. *I brought you to London to tell you I love you.*

Tears sprang into my eyes. Immediately I recalled my childhood wish—for someone to love me enough to fly across the ocean for me. And immediately I knew that the love God has for me is far more meaningful and powerful.

I've told this story dozens of times—each time wiping tears from my eyes. I tell it over and over because it reminds me of who God is: a kind, loving, tender Father who cares for me. A God who hears the desires of my heart, even when they are completely ridiculous. A God who truly loves me—more than I will ever be able to understand.

—ALIZA LATTA

Do you have a story of God's love or care for you that you repeat to others because of the profound impact it had on you?

As humans, we're prone to forget. We may remember an event from our lives a certain way, depending on our feelings at the time or the people involved. Details can become fuzzy, and in the end we fit our memories into a larger story so it makes sense. In his book *Being Mortal*, which is about what matters at the end of life, Atul Gawande writes,

> People seemed to have two different selves—an experiencing self who endures every moment equally and a remembering self who gives almost all the weight of judgment afterward to two single points in time, the worst moment and the last one. The remembering self seems to stick to the Peak-End rule even when the ending is an anomaly. Just a few minutes without pain at the end of their medical procedure dramatically reduced patients' overall pain ratings even after they'd experienced more than half an hour of high level of pain.[2]

Perhaps this is why the Israelites had such a hard time remembering God's mercy in bringing them out of slavery in Egypt and in providing for them in the wilderness. Over and over they complained against Moses, even saying they wished to be back in Egypt (Exod. 16:3). Their remembering selves, of course, did not forget the hardships of slavery, but because that experience ended on the high note of deliverance and provision, perhaps Egypt seemed preferable to their current experiences of hunger and thirst.

However, God was gracious in reminding them of His power and glory and remained present with them through their long journey to the promised land.

In Deuteronomy, Moses warns the next generation to remember what had happened to their parents before them. He urges them to obey the Lord, to love Him, and to remember the commandments He had given them. He tells them, "Repeat them to your children. Talk about them when you sit in your house and when you walk along the road, when you lie down and when you get up" (6:7).

This is how we remember rightly. We tell the same story over and over again so we do not forget the truth.

Forgetting our stories as individuals, as communities, and as a nation can cause us to twist truths into damaging belief systems. How have you seen this happen in your family's history, your church's history, or our nation's history?

Read 1 Samuel 7:7–13. What is the significance of the stone of Ebenezer?

When we don't tell our God-moment stories or repeat the truths He's taught us in the past, we're more prone to lose sight of Him and lose our grasp on our identity. We have many reasons for becoming avid storytellers in the church, but here are two.

The first is simple: we need to tell our stories to remember truth. Storytelling is a sort of living, breathing Ebenezer. It might mean commemorating a significant time of help from God with a piece of jewelry or artwork, then telling the story over and over again. Each time we tell it, we remind ourselves of how He was with us and for us, and anyone who hears it (ourselves included) will be encouraged.

The second reason is to preserve our history and culture. Each person holds within themselves narratives that come from our families, our ethnicities, our communities, and our countries. These narratives have shaped who we are, whether we're aware of it or not. Though not all of us are privileged to have stories from generations past, we can shape the narratives we live now to pass on to the next generation. We can help shape their identities by telling the stories we've lived, giving them a foundation on which to build their own stories.

Do you have stories (good or bad) from your family, culture, community, or church that have shaped you to be the person you are today? If so, what are they?

_____

_____

_____

_____

Our stories have the power to set the path for the future of others. They can act as warning signs for those who may fall into the same temptations or dangers we have. They can be hope for those who don't have anything to hold on to in their current struggle. They can cast a vision for those who can't see all that's possible for them. Our stories can change the world and the many generations that come after us.

But we must also have courage to face the narratives that aren't healthy—wounds from the past that continue to harm others, generational brokenness that continues to plague our families, habits and coping mechanisms that have been learned and shared.

> **Our stories can change the world and the many generations that come after us.**

God is Healer and Redeemer, and He can do both in our lives. May we have the courage to engage with God in retelling the stories we've been given to create new narratives for the generations to come. May we remember and retell what He has done so that others may see the God who loves them and redeems them too.

Do you have a truth or a phrase that has significant meaning between you and God? How will you remind yourself of it? Refer to Deuteronomy 6:8–9 and 1 Samuel 7:12.

How does remembering and retelling narratives about your history and culture require courage from you?

Reflect on this prayer and make it your own today:

Father, when I'm overwhelmed by life and can't see through the fog, it's so easy to forget who You are and who I am in You. Help me to recall my Ebenezer moments to remind myself of how You've been with me and how You've loved me. Give me the courage to face difficult stories from my past in order to change the narrative of my life and the lives of those who come after me. Amen.

They came to Jesus and saw the man who had been demon-possessed, sitting there, dressed and in his right mind; and they were afraid. Those who had seen it described to them what had happened to the demon-possessed man and told about the pigs. Then they began to beg him to leave their region.

As he was getting into the boat, the man who had been demon-possessed begged him earnestly that he might remain with him. Jesus did not let him but told him, "Go home to your own people, and report to them how much the LORD has done for you and how he has had mercy on you." So he went out and began to proclaim in the Decapolis how much Jesus had done for him, and they were all amazed.

Mark 5:15–20

I didn't want to be known as the panic-attack woman. I was writing my first book about learning to rest and was preparing a Bible study to guide others through it, when out of the blue I started experiencing severe anxiety and panic attacks. I was a happily married woman with a loving husband and two adorable children. I was living my childhood dream of becoming a writer and had grown up with a deep faith in God, a love for the Scriptures, and an intimate prayer life.

I had never experienced anxiety before. As the oldest child in a single-parent family, I was the cheerful, optimistic one, taking care of others and putting myself through college. I had served as a missionary and later worked in corporate high tech before becoming a writer.

So I was shocked by the panic attacks I began experiencing and was further surprised to learn that they were caused by emotional PTSD from childhood trauma. My therapist explained that the memories I had carried in my body since I was a child were surfacing because I was now in a safe place to process them. This is how God designed our bodies to work in order to protect us and help us survive.

Working through my trauma was painful, and processing it through writing ended up being healing. At first I was afraid people would misjudge me and think my faith was flawed. I was afraid no one would want to read my book. But it turns out that we all long to know that God cares about the things that have wounded us, that He wants to heal us, and that He has the power to do so.

I never would have guessed during my panic-attack years that I'd later be invited by the US military to be the first civilian to lead a spiritual retreat for army officers. I couldn't have imagined that I'd lead soul care retreats and guide thousands of women to find their belovedness, prioritize their well-being, and rediscover how to choose joy again.

I had been afraid to write about my panic attacks because of what others might think of me, but by writing my story down, by going first to share what had happened to me, God brought healing and freedom to so many others.

It took courage I didn't think I had in me to face my fears and walk the path of healing. But I learned to believe that God's love is made perfect in my weakness, and I will tell that story for as long as I live.

—BONNIE GRAY

How has God used someone's story to bring healing or freedom to you?

_____

_____

_____

_____

We're not told the name of the man who had been demon-possessed, but we read of the evil spirits that tormented him and wrecked his sanity, his life, and his connection to the community. He lived isolated among the tombs, "crying out and cutting himself with stones" (Mark 5:5). Violence, torture, and death lived inside him, and he had no peace or rest. Mark's vivid description sets us up to understand the vast contrast we see after the man's encounter with Jesus.

Our identities are not found in our diseases, our mental health issues, our hardships, or our losses, but those things often guide our stories. Pain (whether visible or invisible), grief, and loss are not the whole of who we are, but they are often the places where we reach the limits of our ability and learn to cry out to God.

When we have little to no evidence for why something is happening, it makes it even harder to understand the point of suffering, and too often there is no logical reason for it. Suffering can leave us feeling isolated and lonely, without the connection to others or even to God that we need to get through it.

But God *is* present and real, particularly through our suffering. He is someone who understands suffering and has written it into the greatest story of love and redemption. Before His resurrection, Jesus was betrayed, cut off from His community, isolated. He suffered and died, and His death wasn't quick. He hung on the cross, bearing the weight of humanity's sin, and was entombed in darkness for three days.

And yet this story of death is the one that gives us hope and life now. Our stories of suffering can do the same for others. They can be portals

God uses to tell His story of power and peace and to assure us of His with-ness.

> **Read Isaiah 53. What words about Jesus stick out to you? How does it encourage you to know that He was "a man of suffering who knew what sickness was" (v. 3)?**

Jesus heals the demon-possessed man by casting the demons out of him and into a large herd of pigs nearby. The pigs plunge to their deaths, drowning in a lake at the bottom of the hill, and the man is left "sitting there, dressed and in his right mind" (Mark 5:15). The man whom the people had once tried to restrain with chains, whom they had seen wandering naked around the tombs screaming, is now sitting quiet and still, clothed, and sane.

Afraid of Jesus's power, the people beg Him to leave their town. They reject Him, but the man who had been healed pleads with Jesus to be allowed into the boat so he can go with Him. And who wouldn't want to be near Jesus after that experience? He wants to stay near the One who has given him life, peace, sanity, and the chance at community once again.

Sometimes we feel closest to God in our hardest seasons of life. When all else has failed, when comfort can't be found in tangible things or in people, when we don't have anything left, we find that God is our anchor, our reason for living, and our hope for tomorrow. And even after the season passes, we wish we could keep feeling God's presence so near to us.

God's nearness doesn't change, but He does ask us to move forward with Him, sharing our stories with others rather than simply staying in that moment of healing or closeness and keeping it to ourselves. Others can enter in through our stories, allowing them access to God in a way they may not have had before.

Psalm 34:18 says God is near to the brokenhearted. How have you seen God in your worst or most painful seasons of life?

_____

_____

_____

_____

When the man healed from demon possession begs to go with Jesus, Jesus replies and says, "Go home to your own people, and report to them how much the Lord has done for you and how he has had mercy on you" (Mark 5:19). Jesus tells him that his testimony will be more powerful if shared with his own people, rather than traveling with Jesus to tell strangers. And the next verse tells us it was so: the man goes out into that region and tells everyone how God had healed him, and they are all amazed by his story (v. 20).

Our stories can bring healing and connection to others and to ourselves. Writing our stories down can reveal truths about ourselves and about God. Like Bonnie experienced, finally putting into words the trauma or grief we've experienced can provide a salve for our wounds.

The same balm can be passed on to others. Our stories are our influence to bring healing, revelation, and wisdom to those who hear them—whether in our immediate communities or shared far and wide on the internet. May we be brave and put into words what God has done in our lives.

> **Our stories are our influence to bring healing, revelation, and wisdom to those who hear them.**

Our stories of healing (or of not being healed) from pain or illness can be scary to tell—particularly when we're telling them for the first time or to people who might not believe us. Read Isaiah 41:10 for encouragement. What story do you feel God nudging you to tell?

_____

_____

_____

_____

Reflect on this prayer and make it your own today:

Lord, You are Healer and the Writer of my story. Even when my prayers for healing are not answered, You are still present and near. I want to tell my stories of You being with me during suffering so others can see You and know You too. Give me the courage to tell stories that are still painful when it is time to tell them, and I pray that lives are changed because of them. Amen.

"If you keep silent at this time, relief and deliverance will come to the Jewish people from another place, but you and your father's family will be destroyed. Who knows, perhaps you have come to your royal position for such a time as this."

Esther sent this reply to Mordecai: "Go and assemble all the Jews who can be found in Susa and fast for me. Don't eat or drink for three days, night or day. I and my female servants will also fast in the same way. After that, I will go to the king even if it is against the law. If I perish, I perish."

Esther 4:14–16

Grace, go up and make the announcement so everyone can hear."

It was common knowledge among my fellow youth group teachers that my voice could travel over the din of students talking and laughing in the fellowship hall. I took a deep breath and bellowed, "QUIET!" Shocked by the volume, the students looked around to see who was talking, only to find the shortest teacher among them telling them to take a seat so we could talk about what to do next.

My voice had always been a bit too loud or a bit too low to be considered "ladylike," according to some adults in my life. They told me I would sound better, nicer, if I spoke a couple of notes higher than my regular alto range. They advised me out of goodwill, but what they didn't realize was that I heard this underlying message in their words: "Your voice isn't normal for a girl. You should speak more quietly or softly because no one's going to like it—or you."

It didn't keep me from speaking at all, but I thought of my voice as "silly" and "manly" and relegated its use to certain situations only. Rallying people together to get things done around the church? Sign me up! But with anything else, I felt like other people's voices were more important, more fit for the job, more necessary than my own.

Only recently, as I began to walk down the path of writing and embarked on my cultural identity journey, have I come to realize that my voice is beautiful in its low tones, powerful in its ability to gather people and have them listen, gentle in its pastoral welcome, and *absolutely* necessary. As a Korean American woman who leads by writing and speaking, it never felt like the time for me to take the stage, so to speak. But in recent years I've seen my voice, my writing, my culture, and current events coming together in a way I hadn't planned for or expected.

My voice is good and is needed just the way it sounds and in the fullness of what makes it mine. For too long the voices of women of color have been silenced or pushed aside as unnecessary, but ears are finally more open and eyes are watching. It's time for me to take the mic and let my voice be heard.

—GRACE P. CHO

In what ways have you found the phrase "for such a time as this" relevant to you?

The book of Esther is a story that has it all. It weaves in romance, action, murder plots, and the underdog winning at the end. It never mentions God's name, but we see how His providential hand is present throughout the story. He guides Esther's life, elevating her to a position she couldn't have gotten by herself.

Esther grew up as an orphan in the care of her cousin Mordecai. They live in Susa, the capital of Persia, as part of the Jewish community that chose not to return to Jerusalem from exile. The Persian king, Xerxes, had gotten rid of his queen for refusing him during a banquet, and as he begins to search for a new queen, he sends for all the beautiful young women in the land. Out of all of them, King Xerxes is captivated by Esther's beauty. He makes her queen, and suddenly her life is completely changed.

The antagonist in the story, Haman, is second in command to the king. Haman hates Mordecai, who refuses to bow to him, and he manipulates the king to make a decree that will exterminate all the Jews in his kingdom. Esther had not revealed her ethnic identity when she became queen, but when Mordecai tells her of Haman's plot to kill, slaughter, and annihilate all of their people, she comes to a crossroads. She must risk her own life by going into the king's presence without being summoned or forfeit the lives of her people by staying silent.

Her ethnicity, her position, and the racial tensions of the day come to a point where she can no longer hide without cost. Mordecai calls her out, saying, "If you keep silent at this time, relief and deliverance will come to the Jewish people from another place, but you and your father's family will be destroyed. Who knows, perhaps you have come to your royal position for such a time as this" (Esther 4:14).

There will be times in life when silence comes at a cost we can't ignore—particularly when it comes to injustice and inequity in our communities. Like Esther, we may face potential harm or even death if we raise our voices, but the cost of being silent will be even greater.

In your own experience, how has keeping silent harmed others, and how has raising your voice protected or helped others?

_____

_____

_____

_____

With position comes responsibility, and the same goes for influence. The more influence we have, the more responsibility we have for others. What is God inviting you to learn, do, or pray about regarding your influence and the responsibility that comes with it?

_____

_____

_____

_____

At this crucial crossroads in her life, Esther could've gone either way. But she tells Mordecai, "Go and assemble all the Jews who can be found in Susa and fast for me. Don't eat or drink for three days, night or day. I and my female servants will also fast in the same way. After that, I will go to the king even if it is against the law. If I perish, I perish" (4:15–16).

Esther responds by leaning in. She leans into fasting and praying, she leans into her community, and she leans fully into her responsibility—even to the point of death: *If I perish, I perish.*

She understands the risk of unveiling her identity as a Jewish woman and the risk for her people, and she decides that it *is* for such a time as this that she has been elevated to her position as queen.

Esther is a foreshadowing of what Jesus does generations later. He considered the risks and the responsibility of loving us and leaned in too—all the way to the cross.

For us, speaking up for others may not necessarily mean risking our physical lives, but it could mean risking our reputations or our relationships. When we come to that crossroads in life where we must choose between safety and risk, we can take heart that we have a spiritual heritage of those who have leaned in, of those who have chosen to lay down their lives for the sake of loving others.

Read Esther 5. How was Esther wise in the way she raised her voice and brought deliverance to her people?

_____

_____

_____

_____

As women of influence, we need wisdom to know how to use our influence and our voices for the sake of others. We need to know ourselves better and be aware of the times we're living in. We need to be abiding in Christ in order to know how the Spirit is moving.

When we're attuned to all these things, we'll be able to recognize as Grace did that we are where we're at, with the people we're with, in the city and church and community we're in, at this point in history, for such a time as this.

> **We need wisdom to know how to use our influence and our voices for the sake of others.**

We don't need to be overwhelmed by the responsibility of influence we carry as followers of Christ, because He is with us. In John 14:26, Jesus promises us that the Holy Spirit will guide us and remind us of everything He's taught us.

Let's be courageous women of influence whose impact can be seen through our love for God and one another—for such a time as this.

Personalize Esther 4:13–14 according to your circumstances.
For example, you can fill in the blanks: *Don't think that you will*
_____ *because you are* _____. *If you keep silent at this*
time, _____. *Who knows, perhaps you have come to*
_____ *for such a time as this.*

Reflect on this prayer and make it your own today:

God, thank You for how You've created us for such a time as
this. When the time comes for us to take a stand and use our
voices and our influence for the sake of others, give us wisdom
and courage to lean in even when the cost is great. Thank You
for loving us so much that You did the same for us. We love You,
Lord. Amen.

notes

Week 4 Be Generous with Your Influence

1. *The NAS New Testament Greek Lexicon*, s.v. "Skorpizo," https://www.biblestudy
tools.com/lexicons/greek/nas/skorpizo.html.

Week 5 Be Intentional with Your Influence

1. Barna Group, "How the Last Decade Changed American Life," July 31, 2013, http://
barna.org/research/how-the-last-decade-changed-american-life/#.Vl3_yt-rTMU; "New Re-
search on the State of Discipleship," December 1, 2015, https://www.barna.com/research
/new-research-on-the-state-of-discipleship/.

2. Barna Group, "State of the Bible 2019: Trends in Engagement," April 18, 2019,
https://www.barna.com/research/state-of-the-bible-2019/.

3. We understand that not all church/faith communities are healthy enough for this to
be possible. We acknowledge that there will be times when it's not safe to lean in and it's
wiser to back away. If you're there now, we ache and lament your reality with you.

Week 6 Tell Your Story

1. Eric Weiner, "Where Heaven and Earth Come Closer," *New York Times*, March 9,
2012, https://www.nytimes.com/2012/03/11/travel/thin-places-where-we-are-jolted-out-of
-old-ways-of-seeing-the-world.html.

2. Atul Gawande, *Being Mortal: Medicine and What Matters in the End* (New York:
Henry Holt, 2015), 237.

about the authors

Grace P. Cho is a Korean American writer, poet, and speaker, and is the editorial manager at (in)courage. She believes telling our stories can change the world and desires to elevate the voices of women of color in the publishing industry. Learn more @gracepcho and at gracepcho.com.

Karina Allen is devoted to helping women live out their unique callings and building authentic community through practical application of Scripture in an approachable, winsome manner. Connect with her on Instagram @karina268.

Lucretia Berry is the creator of Brownicity.com. She is a wife, a mom of three, and a former college professor, whose passion for racial healing led her to author *What LIES Between Us: Fostering First Steps Toward Racial Healing* and to speak at TEDx Charlotte and Q Ideas Charlotte. Find her at brownicity.com and on Instagram @lucretiaberry.

Kaitlyn Bouchillon is a writer who is learning to see God's goodness in the beautiful ordinary of right now. She is the author of *Even If Not: Living, Loving, and Learning in the in Between,* and she'll never turn down an iced latte. Find her at kaitlynbouchillon.com and on Instagram @kaitlyn_bouch.

Dawn Camp is an Atlanta-based photographer, wife, essential oil enthusiast, homeschooling mom to eight, and Mimi to four. She is the author of *It All Began in a Garden* and has edited four book compilations, including *With Love, Mom*. Connect with her at dawncamp.com and on Instagram @dawncamp.

Mary Carver is a writer and speaker who lives for good books, spicy queso, and television marathons—but lives because of God's grace. She writes about giving up on perfect and finding truth in unexpected places at MaryCarver.com and on Instagram @marycarver. Mary and her husband live in Kansas City with their two daughters.

Robin Dance is the author of *For All Who Wander*, is married to her college sweetheart, and is as Southern as sugar-shocked tea. An empty nester with a full life, she's determined to age with grace and laugh at the days to come. Connect with her at robindance.me and on Instagram @robindance.me.

Dorina Lazo Gilmore-Young is a blogger, a speaker, and the author of *Glory Chasers* and *Flourishing Together*. She specializes in helping people navigate grief and flourish in community. An award-winning children's author, Dorina has also served as a journalist, missionary, and social entrepreneur. She and her husband are raising three brave girls. Find her at dorinagilmore.com and on Instagram @dorinagilmore.

Bonnie Gray is a wife, a mom to two boys, and the author of *Whispers of Rest* and *Finding Spiritual Whitespace*. An inspirational speaker who has been featured at Relevant Magazine and Christianity Today, she's guided thousands to detox stress and experience God's love through soul care. Find her at TheBonnieGray.com and on Instagram @thebonniegray.

Tasha Jun is a dreamer, a Hapa girl, wife to Matt, and mama to three little tender warriors. A coffee-drinker, storyteller, and kimchi-eater, she was made to walk where cultures collide, on dirt roads and carefully placed cobblestone streets. Jesus is her heartbeat. Find her on Instagram @tashajunb and at tashajun.com.

Becky Keife loves serving as the community manager for (in)courage. She is the author of *No Better Mom for the Job* and is also a speaker, editor, and blessed mama of three spirited boys. Connect with her on Instagram @beckykeife.

Aliza Latta is a Canadian writer, journalist, and artist, who is a huge fan of telling stories. She writes about faith and young adulthood at alizalatta.com and is the author of the novel *Come Find Me, Sage Parker*. Find her on Instagram @alizalatta.

Anna Rendell is the (in)courage digital content manager and lives in Minnesota with her husband and three kids. She loves a good book and a great latte. Anna is the author of *Pumpkin Spice for Your Soul* and *A Moment of Christmas*. Visit her at AnnaRendell.com and on Instagram @annaerendell.

Bible Studies to Refresh Your Soul

In these six-week Bible studies, your friends at (in)courage will help you dive deep into real-life issues, the transforming power of God's Word, and what it means to courageously live your faith.

100 Days of Hope and Peace

In this 100-day devotional, the (in)courage community reaches into the grief and pain of both crisis and ordinary life. Each day includes a key Scripture, a heartening devotion, and a prayer to remind you that God is near and hope is possible. You won't find tidy bows or trite quick fixes, just arrows pointing you straight to Jesus.

(in)courage welcomes you

to a place where authentic, brave women connect deeply with God and others. Through the power of shared stories and meaningful resources, (in)courage champions women and celebrates the strength Jesus gives to live out our calling as God's daughters. Together we build community, celebrate diversity, and **become women of courage**.

Join us at **www.incourage.me**
& connect with us on social media!